YOUR DMV STUDY BUDDY

CALIFORNIA EDITION

DRIVER LICENSE

ID: 123-456-789-10

DOB: DD/MM/YYYY   ISS: DD/MM/YYYY

EXP: DD/MM/YYYY

NAME SURNAME

CLASS:

SEX   WGT
HGT   EYES

GET READY TO NAIL THE DMV TEST

NAIL YOUR TEST PUBLISHING

Author's Note

Please be advised that the State of California requires everyone to study the Official Driver License Handbook. You can easily download it through the QR code below:

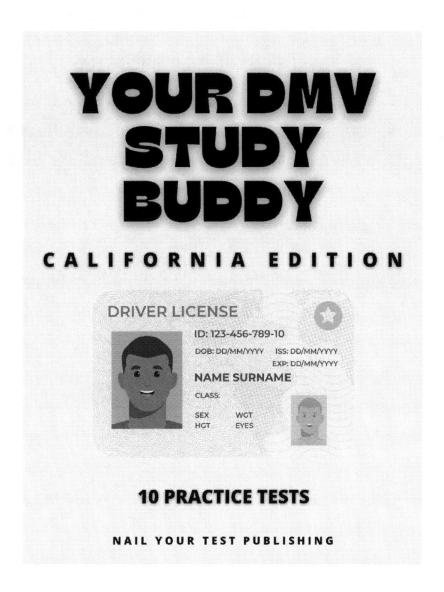

YOUR DMV STUDY BUDDY

CALIFORNIA EDITION

DRIVER LICENSE

ID: 123-456-789-10

DOB: DD/MM/YYYY   ISS: DD/MM/YYYY

EXP: DD/MM/YYYY

NAME SURNAME

CLASS:

SEX   WGT
HGT   EYES

10 PRACTICE TESTS

NAIL YOUR TEST PUBLISHING

Dear reader, to make the most of your book we have included 10 practice tests to familiarize even more with the rules of the road. To download this free resource scan the QR code below.

Table of Contents

1 Introduction

Welcome to *Your DMV Study Buddy – California Edition*, your friendly guide to confidently navigating the highways and byways of the Golden State! This guide is a fantastic study tool for the DMV test, but it's so much more than that. It aims to equip you with the knowledge you need to be a responsible and skilled driver. Whether you're a newbie revving to get on the road or a seasoned pro after a refresher, this manual is your perfect pit stop. So, without further ado, let's buckle up and explore the thrilling world of driving in California together!

1.1 Understanding Traffic Laws and Regulations

To be a conscientious driver, it's crucial to have a thorough understanding of traffic laws and regulations. In this guide, we'll delve into the various traffic laws that keep California's roads orderly, including traffic signs and signals, speed limits, and right-of-way rules. By getting to grips with these laws, you'll be confidently zipping through intersections, smoothly changing lanes, and making well-informed decisions behind the wheel.

1.2 Importance of Safe Driving

Safe driving is more than just a responsibility; it's a pledge to ensure your safety, that of your passengers, and everyone else out on the road. In this guide, we spotlight the importance of safe driving habits and offer you valuable insights on defensive driving, maintaining adequate following distances, and staying alert on the road. We'll also explore specifics such as distracted driving, impaired driving, and the crucial role of seat belts and child restraints. Together, we'll foster a safety-first mentality that can contribute to a positive driving culture in California. Remember, driving isn't just about getting from point A to point B—it's about making the roads safer for all of us. So, strap in, flip the page, and let's kick off this enlightening and exhilarating journey together!

2 Obtaining a California Driver's License

2.1 Eligibility and Requirements

So, you're ready to hit the scenic routes of California and start your driving journey. Before you can rev up and roll out, you'll need to meet some eligibility criteria and fulfill certain requirements. Let's dig in:

Eligibility: To kick things off, to be eligible for a driver's license in California, you must be at least 16 years old. If you're under 18, you'll need to have had your provisional permit for at least six months without any traffic violations before you can apply for a driver's license..

Requirements: Let's go over the requirements to get your hands on that coveted driver's license. We'll go into detail on each aspect later in this guide, but here's the snapshot:

- **Gather Required Documents:** You'll need to submit documents that prove your identity, residency, and Social Security number. This could be your birth certificate or passport, evidence of your residential address (like utility bills or lease agreements), and your Social Security card.

- **Complete Driver Education and Training:** For new drivers, especially those under 17 and a half, California requires completion of a state-approved driver education course. This course will teach you about California traffic laws, safe driving practices, and the hazards of impaired driving.

- **Pass the Written Knowledge Test:** Next, it's time to ace the written knowledge test. This test evaluates your understanding of traffic laws, road signs, and safe driving practices.

- **Pass the Vision Exam:** As part of the application process, you'll need to take a vision exam to ensure your eyesight meets the necessary standards for driving.

- **Ace the Driving Skills Test:** Once you've tackled the above requirements, it's time to show off your driving skills. You'll need to schedule and pass a behind-the-wheel driving test, which includes a practical driving examination. This test evaluates your ability to operate a vehicle safely and adhere to traffic rules.

- **Pay the Required Fees:** Last but not least, you'll need to cough up the necessary fees for obtaining your driver's license. These fees cover processing your application and issuing your license. We'll dive into the specifics of the fees later.

And that's a wrap! By satisfying the eligibility criteria, gathering the required documents, completing the necessary education and exams, and paying the fees, you'll be cruising down the highway towards obtaining your driver's license in California.

2.2 Types of Licenses

Alright, let's take a peek at the variety of licenses you can get in sunny California. The Golden State offers a range of options for newbies, seasoned drivers, commercial operators, and everyone in between.

- **Class C Driver's License:** The Class C license is the standard "driver's license" in California. It allows you to operate most everyday vehicles, such as cars, SUVs, and trucks. After you meet the eligibility criteria and pass the relevant tests, this license is yours!
- **Provisional Permit:** If you're a budding driver who is at least 15 1/2 years old, you can apply for a provisional permit in California. With this permit, you can start practicing your driving skills with certain restrictions, like having a licensed adult 25 years old or older with you at all times.
- **Commercial Driver's License (CDL):** If driving big rigs or buses is your thing, you'll need a Commercial Driver's License. The CDL comes with a bit more responsibility – you'll have to pass additional tests specific to commercial driving. There are different classes of CDLs, depending on the type and size of the vehicle you'll be operating.
- **Motorcycle License (Class M1 or M2):** For the motorcycle enthusiasts out there, California offers Class M1 and M2 motorcycle licenses. To get these, you'll need to pass a written test and a separate driving test specifically for motorcycle operation. These licenses open the way for your two-wheel adventures on Californian roads!
- **CDL Endorsements:** If you're planning on operating specific types of commercial vehicles, you may need to add endorsements to your CDL. These can range from a school bus or tanker endorsement to a hazardous materials (HazMat) endorsement, each requiring additional testing.
- **Special Certificates:** If you need to operate certain vehicles or offer specific transportation services, California offers special certificates. These are for drivers

of vehicles like school buses, farm labor vehicles, and more. Each one has its own unique requirements and might need extra training or testing.

When you're choosing the right license for your needs, think about what you'll be driving and what your goals are. You can always check out the California Driver Handbook and consult the California Department of Motor Vehicles (DMV) for more detailed information and specific requirements. Once you've decided, you'll be one step closer to cruising down California's highways and byways.

2.3 Provisional Permit Regulations

If you're a young Californian ready to taste the freedom of the open road, your first step is getting your Provisional Permit. It's like a mini-milestone that lets you gather some essential driving experience, albeit with a few rules and regulations. So let's get into it!

- **Age Requirement:** To apply for a Provisional Permit in California, you have to be at least 15 1/2 years old. If you're a teen itching to hop in the driver's seat, it's time to gear up!
- **Parental Consent:** For those under 18, you'll need parental or guardian consent to get your Provisional Permit. Your parents or guardians will play a critical role as they'll guide and supervise your initial driving experiences.
- **Driver Education Course:** Remember when I mentioned that learning part? Well, here it is again. To get your Provisional Permit, you'll need to complete a Driver Education course.
- **Supervised Driving:** Once you have your Provisional Permit, you can start practicing driving, but don't forget your co-pilot! You'll need a licensed adult who is at least 25 years old in the car with you at all times when you're driving. Yes, this means no solo rides just yet!
- **Nighttime and Passenger Restrictions**: As a new driver with a Provisional Permit, there are certain rules you need to keep in mind. For the first year, you're not allowed to drive between 11 PM and 5 AM. Also, you can't have passengers under 20 years old in the car, unless accompanied by a licensed parent, guardian, instructor, or a licensed adult over 25.
- **Practice, Practice, Practice:** Your Provisional Permit is your golden ticket to accumulate precious driving experience. Use this time to polish your driving skills, learn traffic laws inside out, and develop safe driving habits. Remember, practice makes perfect, and the more practice you have, the more confident and prepared you'll be when you go for the gold - your driver's license!

- **Knowledge and Skills Tests:** Once you've honed your skills and think you're ready, you can schedule and take the knowledge and skills tests to get your driver's license. Studying the California Driver Handbook and putting in lots of practice are the keys to acing these tests.

By following these Provisional Permit rules, you're well on your way to becoming a proficient, responsible driver. It's an exciting journey, full of new experiences and growth, so soak it all in and enjoy the ride!

2.4 Required Documentation

The journey towards getting your driver's license needs some paperwork. Let's delve into what the Golden State needs from you:

- **Proof of Identity:** Starting off, you need to establish your identity. You can use your birth certificate, valid passport, or other acceptable forms of ID to do this. These documents authenticate your identity and ensure that your license is issued in the right name.
- **Proof of California Residency:** California requires you to confirm your residential address. You can do this using documents like utility bills, rental agreements, or a mortgage statement. Make sure the documents have your name and address on them, so your residency can be verified. And, don't worry if you're still living with your parents. You can provide a document with your parent or guardian's address, along with a statement from them verifying you reside at the same address. This can be known as a Certification of Address form. Along with this, you'll still need a second proof of residential address. If you don't have a second document under your name, don't sweat it. Your parent or guardian can present another document under their name as the second proof of address. This could be a recent utility bill, a bank statement, or any other document listed under the acceptable proofs on the California Department of Motor Vehicles (DMV) website.
- **Social Security Number (SSN):** You also need to provide your Social Security number (SSN). This helps the state maintain your driving records and ensures proper identification. You can present your Social Security card, W-2 form, or other official documents with your SSN.
- **Proof of Citizenship or Legal Presence:** If you're a U.S. citizen, your birth certificate or valid passport can serve as proof of citizenship. If you're not a U.S. citizen, you'll need to provide proof of your legal presence in the United States. This can include documents like a permanent resident card or Employment Authorization Document (EAD).

- **Completion of Driver's Education:** Before applying for a driver's license in California, you must complete an approved driver's education course.

Do note that these are general requirements and additional documentation may be needed based on your specific circumstances. It's always smart to check the California DMV website or get in touch with their office for the most recent and accurate details.

So, gear up, my friend, and gather all the necessary documents before heading to the driver's license office. It's going to make your process smoother and help you get your license without any hitches.

2.5 Written, Vision, and Road Tests

Before you can cruise California's beautiful roads, you must prove that you have the necessary knowledge, vision, and driving skills. So, how do you do that? Let's get into the specifics:

- **Written Test:** This test, also known as the knowledge test, is your first hurdle. It gauges your understanding of traffic laws, road signs, and safe driving practices. A thorough study of the California Driver's Handbook will help you ace this test, which covers a wide array of topics, such as traffic rules, road signs, right-of-way, and safe driving techniques.
  The test itself comprises 46 multiple-choice questions divided into two parts. The first part, with 36 questions, focuses on road rules. Here you'll be tested on your knowledge of California's traffic laws, safe driving practices, and the different types of traffic signs and their meanings.
  The second part, containing 10 questions, is all about road signs. This section assesses your familiarity with various traffic signs, signals, and pavement markings. To pass, you'll need to score at least 83%, meaning you must get a minimum of 38 questions correct in total.
  Preparation is key. So, study this book thoroughly, but also remember to refer to the official California Driver Handbook, the ultimate guide for your exam.
- **Vision Test:** Good vision is crucial for safe driving. As part of the vision test, an examiner will assess your visual acuity to ensure it meets the required standards. You'll be asked to read a series of letters or numbers from a vision chart. If you wear glasses or contacts, remember to bring them for the test.
- **Road Test:** After you've successfully passed the written and vision tests, it's time for the road test. This is when you demonstrate your practical driving skills under the observation of a licensed examiner. They will evaluate your ability to control

the vehicle, follow traffic rules, and execute various maneuvers such as turning, parking, and merging. Practice your driving skills in advance and prepare for different scenarios you might encounter on the road.

Remember, these tests are designed to ensure your safety and the safety of others on the road. So approach them with confidence, clear understanding of the rules, and ample practice. Don't hesitate to ask questions if you're unsure about anything. With preparation and focus, you'll soon be ready to enjoy the freedom and responsibility of driving.

2.6 Driver's License Fees

We're nearing the end of our journey. As you prepare to hit the roads of California, it's important to be aware of the various fees involved in obtaining a driver's license. Although fees may not be the most exciting topic, consider them your financial contribution towards maintaining the safety and quality of California's roads and services.

- **Application Fee:** When you apply for a driver's license in California, there's an application fee you'll need to pay. This fee covers the administrative costs of processing your application. The exact amount can vary, so always check the current fee schedule on the California Department of Motor Vehicles (DMV) website.
- **License Fee:** Besides the application fee, there's a separate fee for the driver's license itself. This fee covers the costs of producing and issuing your license. Like the application fee, the license fee can vary based on several factors. It's crucial to bring an acceptable payment method, such as cash, check, or credit card, when you visit the DMV office.
- **Other Services and Endorsements:** Depending on your specific needs, there may be additional fees for certain services or endorsements. For instance, if you're adding a motorcycle endorsement to your driver's license or applying for a commercial driver's license (CDL), there may be extra fees associated with those processes. Once again, always consult the DMV website for the most current information on fees.

Bear in mind that fees can change over time, so it's essential to stay informed about the current fee schedule. Detailed fee information can be found on the DMV website or by contacting their office directly.

Your driver's license fees help support the administration and upkeep of California's driver's licensing system, contributing to the resources and services provided by the DMV to ensure the safety and efficiency of the state's roads.

So, as you gear up to get your driver's license in California, make sure to budget for the application fee, license fee, and any additional fees that may apply to your specific situation. Being informed and having the necessary funds on hand will ensure a smooth completion of the process. Good luck!

3 Driver Safety

3.1 Seat Belt and Child Restraint Laws

When we think about road safety in California, seat belts and child restraints come up as the unsung heroes. We all get the significance of securing ourselves and our kids, but let's dig a bit deeper into California's seat belt and child restraint laws:

Imagine this scenario: you're all set to start your sunny California road trip, and just before you hit the road, you ensure everyone's buckled up. It's a quick yet vital step that could save lives and prevent injuries.

In the Golden State, seat belt laws have been set up to protect drivers and passengers of all ages.

- **Seat Belt Requirements:** California law is crystal clear about this - every single person in the car, regardless of where they're seated, needs to be wearing a seat belt. It doesn't matter whether you're driving or just enjoying the journey as a passenger. The rule of thumb is: seat belts are always a must. Think of them as a comforting, secure hug that keeps you safe in case of an unexpected halt or crash.
- **Child Restraint Laws:** Now, for the little munchkins, California has set very specific safety regulations. Children under the age of eight are required to be strapped in a federally approved child restraint system. That's car seats that match their age, weight, and height. Consider it a specialized safety bubble for our little adventurers, shielding them from any harm.
- **Booster Seats**: If your kid is between eight years old or until they reach a height of 4'9", they need to be sitting in a booster seat, unless they meet the height and weight requirements for a standard seat belt. Booster seats give them the extra lift they need to ensure the seat belt fits properly, providing additional protection if an accident were to occur.

Seat belt and child restraint laws aren't just some pesky rules to follow—they're about securing the safety and welfare of everyone on the road. By ensuring we buckle up and our kids are correctly strapped in, we minimize the risk of serious injuries and increase our chances of walking away unscathed from a collision.

So let's remember, seat belts are like our faithful travel partners—they're there to protect us every step of the way. So, let's buckle up, take the road, and make the most of our journey, all the while keeping safety our top priority.

3.2 Airbags Laws in California

While we're on the topic of road safety, let's take a moment to chat about another lifesaving device: airbags. In California, there are some pretty clear-cut rules about these handy, protective features. Let's dive in:

Picture this: you're cruising down the Pacific Coast Highway, soaking in the breathtaking ocean views. Suddenly, a car pulls out in front of you unexpectedly. You hit the brakes, but it's too late to avoid a collision. It's in these split seconds that your vehicle's airbags become the unsung heroes, inflating rapidly to cushion you from the impact.

In sunny California, there are laws set up to ensure airbags are doing their job effectively:

- **Airbag Requirements:** Every car registered in California must be equipped with federally approved airbags. No matter whether you're behind the wheel or in the passenger seat, these airbags serve as a crucial barrier between you and potential harm during a collision.
- **Airbag Tampering and Fraud:** It's a no-brainer, but in California, tampering with airbags is a serious offense. And by tampering, we mean anything from intentionally disabling them to selling or installing counterfeit airbags. If you're buying a used car, be vigilant and have a trusted mechanic check to ensure the airbags are genuine and functioning as they should. It's always better to be safe than sorry, right?
- **Airbag Maintenance:** Just like you'd maintain other parts of your vehicle, it's crucial to keep your airbags in top condition. If your airbag warning light comes on, don't ignore it. Seek professional help ASAP because it might mean there's a problem with your airbags, and you definitely want those working properly.

Remember, airbags, like seat belts, are your car's bodyguards—they're there to protect you when things take an unexpected turn on the road. Let's value them, keep them in check, and carry on with our Californian journeys with peace of mind, knowing we've got our trusty airbags on standby."

3.3 Defensive Driving

Now that we've chatted about seat belts, child restraints, and airbags, let's move onto another important aspect of California road safety - defensive driving. It's not as complicated as it sounds, I promise! So, buckle up as we take a trip down the highways and byways of defensive driving in California.

Think of it like this: you're on the 405 during rush hour. It's a jungle out there with cars zipping in and out, pedestrians, cyclists, and even the occasional palm tree swaying in the wind. That's where defensive driving comes into play. It's all about anticipating potential dangers and making safe decisions on the road.

Here are a few pointers to keep in mind:

- **Stay Alert:** In California, from the crowded streets of LA to the more laid-back roads of Big Sur, being alert is a key part of defensive driving. Always keep your eyes on the road, your hands on the wheel, and your mind on the task at hand. It's like being a road warrior, always ready for whatever comes your way.
- **Anticipate Others:** Here's a hot tip - don't just focus on your own driving; keep an eye out for other drivers too. Not everyone follows the rules, and sometimes you might find yourself next to a driver who thinks they're in the Fast & Furious. Defensive driving is about anticipating their actions and adjusting accordingly to keep things safe.
- **Keep a Safe Distance:** Tailgating is a big no-no in the defensive driving rulebook. Always maintain a safe distance from the vehicle in front of you. It's not a race; it's about ensuring everyone gets to their destination safely.
- **Take a Defensive Driving Course:** Even if you think you're the best driver in California, a defensive driving course can be a real eye-opener. Not only can it potentially save you on auto insurance or help shave points off your driving record, but it will also equip you with skills to navigate the roads safely.

Defensive driving isn't just a set of guidelines—it's a mindset. It's about taking responsibility for our safety and the safety of others on the road. After all, we're all in this together, navigating the beautiful and diverse roads of California. So, let's drive defensively, protect each other, and keep the Golden State's roads as safe as they can be."

3.4 Distracted Driving

Alright, let's shift gears and chat about something that's a serious issue not only in California but on roads everywhere - distracted driving. It's a topic that's worth discussing, especially as our lives become increasingly connected, and our attention often gets pulled in several directions at once.

Picture this: You're cruising down Route 101, the ocean on one side, rolling hills on the other, and your favorite song comes on the radio. You reach for your phone to share the moment on social media. But hang on a second, that's a classic example of distracted driving. It's moments like these that California's laws are designed to prevent.

Let's break it down:

- **No Handheld Devices:** In California, it's illegal to hold a cell phone or electronic device while driving. That's right, no texting, calling, or even holding your phone at a stoplight. So, that perfect California sunset snapshot will have to wait until you've safely parked your car.
- **Hands-Free Only:** If you absolutely need to use your phone, make sure you're using a hands-free device, like a Bluetooth headset, voice command function, or a dashboard mount. But remember, even hands-free isn't risk-free. It's always safer to make calls or send texts before or after your journey.
- **Teen Drivers:** For drivers under 18, it's even stricter. California law prohibits them from using any kind of mobile device while driving, even if it's hands-free. The focus for new drivers should always be 100% on the road.

Keep Distractions to a Minimum: This isn't just about mobile devices. Eating, grooming, fiddling with your GPS, or even turning around to chat with passengers can all take your focus off the road. When you're behind the wheel, driving should be your number one priority.

In the end, distracted driving isn't worth it. Not only are you risking a hefty fine, but more importantly, you're risking your safety and the safety of others on the road. So next time you're enjoying California's scenic drives, remember to keep distractions to a minimum and your focus on the road. After all, the best way to enjoy the journey is to arrive safely at your destination.

3.5 Impaired Driving: Alcohol and Drugs

As we continue our chat about road safety in the Golden State, let's turn our attention to a serious and often tragic issue: impaired driving due to alcohol and drugs. This isn't a light topic by any means, but it's an important one to address.

Let's lay out a scene: Imagine you're celebrating a friend's birthday at a beach bar in Santa Monica. You've had a few drinks and you're feeling good. It might seem like no big deal to get behind the wheel and drive home, right? Wrong. This is where impaired driving laws come into play in California.

Here's the lowdown:

- **Blood Alcohol Concentration (BAC):** In California, it's illegal to drive with a BAC of 0.08% or higher if you're 21 or older. For commercial drivers, the limit is even lower at 0.04%. And if you're under 21, the state has a zero-tolerance policy, meaning any measurable amount of alcohol is grounds for a DUI.
- **Drugs:** And it's not just about alcohol. Driving under the influence of drugs (and this includes legal drugs or prescription medication if they impair your ability to drive) is also a criminal offense. That's right, whether it's marijuana, prescription meds, or illegal substances, if it impairs your driving, it's a no-go.
- **DUI Checkpoints:** Law enforcement in California frequently sets up DUI checkpoints to ensure the safety of all drivers on the road. So remember, getting caught driving under the influence carries severe penalties, including fines, license suspension, and even jail time.
- **Rideshare and Designated Drivers:** Luckily, we live in an era where options like Uber, Lyft, and good old-fashioned designated drivers are readily available. These alternatives are always a smarter, safer choice than getting behind the wheel when you're not 100% sober.

Impaired driving isn't just illegal—it's downright dangerous. It's about your safety, the safety of your passengers, and everyone else sharing California's roads. So let's be responsible, make smart choices, and remember: there's no shame in handing over the keys if you've been partying.

3.6 Drowsy Driving

Time for us to address another serious, yet often overlooked aspect of road safety - drowsy driving. Trust me, it's just as dangerous as it sounds. After all, falling asleep at the wheel in California's diverse landscape can have serious consequences.

Let's paint a picture: You've been exploring the sights and sounds of San Francisco all day, and now it's time to drive back to your place in LA. You're tired but figure you can power through the sleepiness. Wrong move. That's precisely the kind of scenario where drowsy driving sneaks up on you.

Here's what you need to know:

- **The Dangers:** Drowsy driving is similar to drunk driving. Seriously! Lack of sleep slows your reaction time, impairs your decision-making skills, and increases the chances of an accident. It's like trying to navigate the busy I-5 with a blindfold on. Not a good idea, right?

- **Signs to Look Out For:** Yawning, heavy eyelids, wandering thoughts, missing traffic signs, or drifting from your lane are all signs that you're too tired to drive. If you notice these, it's time to pull over for a power nap or switch drivers if possible.
- **Prevention:** The best way to avoid drowsy driving is pretty straightforward - get enough sleep, especially before long drives. Also, plan breaks into your trip. A good rule of thumb is to take a break every two hours or 100 miles. Grab a snack, stretch your legs, or even take a quick nap.
- **California Law:** While there's no specific law against drowsy driving in California as of my knowledge cutoff in September 2021, causing an accident due to fatigue could lead to reckless driving charges. Plus, commercial drivers have specific regulations regarding rest periods to prevent drowsy driving.

In a state as beautiful as California, we all want to take in as much as we can. But remember, it's not worth sacrificing sleep and safety. Always prioritize rest before hitting the road, and if you feel tired while driving, don't hesitate to pull over and take a break. Safety first, adventures second.

3.7 Aggressive Driving and Road Rage

Let's be honest, we've all likely experienced at one point or another - aggressive driving and road rage. It's a less-than-pleasant part of driving, but an important topic to discuss nonetheless.

Imagine this: You're cruising along the iconic Highway 1, soaking in those spectacular California coastline views when suddenly a car cuts you off. Instantly, your heart rate speeds up, your grip tightens on the steering wheel, and you're tempted to honk your horn or shout a choice word or two. Yep, that's road rage creeping in.

So, what's the 411 on this?
- **Know the Difference:** First, it's essential to differentiate between aggressive driving and road rage. Aggressive driving can include speeding, tailgating, or running red lights - basically, it's reckless, but not necessarily personal. Road rage, on the other hand, is a step further. It's an angry, violent reaction towards another driver, which can lead to dangerous situations.
- **Cool it Down:** If you find yourself getting heated behind the wheel, take some deep breaths and try to cool down. After all, getting angry at another driver isn't going to do anything except raise your blood pressure. Plus, the other driver might not even realize they've done something to upset you.

- **Keep Your Distance:** If you encounter an aggressive driver or someone showing signs of road rage, the best thing to do is keep your distance. You don't want to provoke them further, so don't engage, and if necessary, change your route to avoid a confrontation.
- **Laws and Penalties:** While there may not be specific "road rage" laws in place, aggressive driving can lead to tickets for speeding, reckless driving, or other traffic violations. In some severe cases, it could even result in criminal charges. So, remember, it's just not worth it.

At the end of the day, we're all just trying to get from A to B safely. So, let's do our part to keep California's roads chill. Take a deep breath, crank up those beach vibes, and remember: we're all in this together, sharing the road. Drive cool, California!

4 Rules of the Road

4.1 Pavement Markings

Ah, pavement markings—the colorful lines and symbols that guide us on our journey. Have you ever noticed those painted markings on the roads in California? They're not just there for decoration—they serve an important purpose. Let's see it.

Imagine driving down the road, and you see those white and yellow lines stretching out ahead. Those are pavement markings, my friend, and they're like little road communicators. They provide valuable information to help us navigate the roads safely and efficiently.

Edge Lines

Those lines that run along the sides of the pavement. You might have noticed them during your drives, and they serve an important purpose.

Let's break it down:

1. **White Edge Lines:** You'll often see solid white lines along the right side of the road. These lines act as a boundary, indicating the edge of the travel lane. They let us know that we should stay within our lane and avoid drifting too close to the shoulder or the edge of the road. It's a friendly reminder to maintain our position on the road and avoid any unexpected surprises.

2. **Yellow Edge Lines:** Now, let's talk about the yellow lines. You might spot solid yellow lines along the left side of the road. These lines serve a similar purpose—to mark the edge of the travel lane. They're typically seen on divided roads or highways, indicating the boundary between opposing lanes of traffic. They help us maintain a safe distance from oncoming traffic and ensure a smooth flow of vehicles.

3. **Dashed Edge Lines:** Sometimes, you'll come across dashed white or yellow lines along the edges of the road. These dashed lines are usually seen in areas where lane changes are allowed, such as entrance or exit ramps, or where merging or turning movements are expected. They provide guidance and help us navigate these transitional zones safely.

The main purpose of these white and yellow edge lines is to provide visual cues, helping us maintain our position on the road and promoting safe driving habits. By staying within the lines, we can avoid drifting off the road or encroaching into opposing lanes, reducing the risk of accidents.

White Lane Lines

First things first: white lane lines separate lanes of traffic moving in the same direction. But not all white lane lines are born equal.

- **Dashed White Lines**: When you encounter dashed white lines on the road, it means you have the freedom to change lanes if it's safe to do so. These lines provide opportunities for lane changes, such as when merging onto a highway or passing a slower-moving vehicle. Just make sure to use your signals, check your blind spots, and make the maneuver safely.

- **Solid White Lines:** solid white lines tell a different story. When you see solid white lines on the road, it means you should stay within your lane unless you must do so to avoid a hazard. These lines are like gentle reminders, guiding you to maintain your position and preventing unnecessary lane changes. Solid white lines indicate that it's generally unsafe to change lanes in that particular area.

- **Double Solid White Lines**: they're like an invisible wall. When you encounter double solid white lane lines on the road, it means you should not change lanes. These lines act as a clear indication that lane changes are not allowed in that particular area. It's a way to ensure the flow of traffic remains steady and predictable, reducing the chances of accidents or confusion.

Yellow Lane Lines

Imagine this: you're cruising down a California highway, and you see those eye-catching yellow lines guiding you along the way. Those lines are like little rays of sunshine, playing a vital role in keeping our roads safe and organized.

Let's explore the significance of yellow lane lines:

- **Single Broken Yellow Line:** the single broken yellow line is like a reminder to proceed with caution and be flexible on the road. It indicates that passing is allowed if it's safe and legal to do so. It's like a little invitation to make a maneuver—whether it's passing a slower vehicle or changing lanes—when it's appropriate and safe.

- **Double Solid Yellow Line:** no Passing Zone. When you encounter a double solid yellow line, it means no passing is allowed. These lines act as a clear indication that it's unsafe to overtake or pass another vehicle in that specific area. They're like a visual barrier, urging you to stay in your lane and maintain a safe distance from oncoming traffic.

- **Double yellow lines—solid on right ("your side" of line), broken on left:** passing is not allowed. Be aware cars driving in the opposite direction may pass the car in front of them.

- **Double yellow lines—broken on right ("your side" of line), solid on left:** passing is allowed when it's safe to do so. Cars driving in the opposite direction are not granted this possibility.

Turn Lanes

Arrows are often used with white lane lines to show which turn may be made from the lane. Pretty straightforward, right?

- Lane is marked with a curved arrow and the word "ONLY": you must turn in the direction of the arrow.

- Lane is marked with both a curved and straight arrow: you may either turn or go straight.

- Two-way roadway with center lane: drivers from either direction may use the center lane for left turns; you must not use for passing.

Reversible Lanes

Some highways have reversible traffic lanes to help handle rush-hour traffic. The direction of traffic is normally reversed at set times each day. These lanes are marked with special pavement markings, lane signals, and signs.

Bicycle Lanes

Some roads have pavement markings that show lanes specifically designated for the exclusive use of bicycles or for shared use.

- **Exclusive bike lane:** solid white lines separate these bike lanes from motor vehicle travel lanes. Often marked with bike lane signs/symbols.

- **Shared-use lane:** marked with "sharrows." These markings alert motorists that bicyclists may use the entire lane, indicate to bicyclists where to ride, and discourage bicycling in the wrong direction.

White Stop Lines

Stop lines show where you must stop for a stop sign or red light. You must stop your vehicle before any part of it crosses the line before the crosswalk.

Crosswalks

Marked with solid white lines and sometimes filled with white diagonal or perpendicular lines. Shows where pedestrians should cross. Motorists must always yield the right-of-way to pedestrians in a crosswalk.

Other Markings

- Curbs are often marked yellow in no parking zones near fire hydrants or intersections.
- Yellow or white diagonal stripes mark fixed obstructions (medians, no parking zones, etc.).
- It is illegal to park in or drive through areas that have pavement markings indicating fire lanes or safety zones.

4.2 Traffic Signs

Traffic sign colors

Alright, let's talk about traffic sign colors in California! Believe it or not, the colors aren't chosen just to complement our beautiful sunsets. Each hue has a specific meaning, helping you understand the rules of the road and navigate safely. Plus, who said learning can't be colorful?

- Let's kick things off with the universal "stop" color: **red**. In California, as in the rest of the world, red signals STOP! It's used for stop signs, yield signs, and prohibitions – anything that's not allowed on the road. So if you see a red sign, it's time to hit the brakes or pay close attention.
- **Green** is your go-to color for directions and permitted movements. Often seen on highway guide signs, it tells you which lane to choose for your exit or what directions are available from each lane.
- **Blue** signs are all about services and amenities. Need a hospital, rest stop, or an EV charging station? Look out for blue signs!
- Then there's **yellow**, the color of caution. In California, yellow signs warn you about potential hazards or changes in road conditions, like sharp turns, merges, or pedestrian crossings. It's not just the color of our sunshine, but a heads-up to stay alert.
- Next, let's talk **orange**. Orange is the color Californians see when road work or construction is ahead. Spot an orange sign? It's time to slow your roll and be prepared for possible changes in road conditions.
- **White**, often combined with black, red, or green, is used on regulatory signs. These are the ones that tell you the do's and don'ts of the road, like speed limits, "No U-Turn" commands, and other traffic regulations.
- Last, but not least, there's **brown**. Brown signs guide you to public recreation areas or cultural sites. If you're hunting for the next state park or a historical marker, follow the brown signs.

So there you have it! In California, traffic sign colors are a vital part of our road communication system, providing clear, crucial information to drivers. So, on your next cruise down the Pacific Coast Highway or trip to the Sierras, take note of the sign colors. They're speaking to you in a language all drivers should understand!

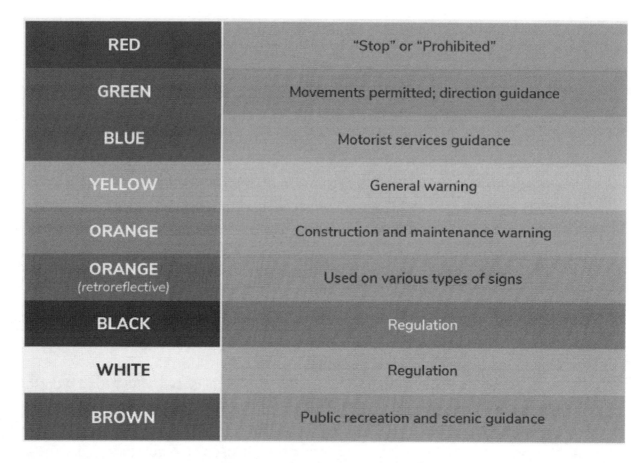

RED	"Stop" or "Prohibited"
GREEN	Movements permitted; direction guidance
BLUE	Motorist services guidance
YELLOW	General warning
ORANGE	Construction and maintenance warning
ORANGE (retroreflective)	Used on various types of signs
BLACK	Regulation
WHITE	Regulation
BROWN	Public recreation and scenic guidance

Figure 1: Traffic Sign Colors[1]

Traffic sign shapes

Shifting gears from colors to shapes, eh? I'm ready! Just like their colorful counterparts, the shapes of traffic signs in California carry significant meaning. These aren't chosen by any aesthetic standard, but to convey specific types of information. The shapes are fairly universal across the United States, but a recap never hurts, right?

- Let's start with the unique **octagon** shape. It's exclusive to stop signs. This distinct shape is easily recognizable, even in low visibility situations, making it universally understood as a symbol to halt.
- Next up, the most frequent flier on our roads: the **rectangle**. These come in two orientations - vertical or horizontal. Vertical rectangles are usually regulatory signs like speed limits or specific instructions, such as "no turn on red". Horizontal rectangles, however, often serve as guide signs, offering directions, distances, and destination markers.

---

[1] https://driversed.com/trending/california-road-signs-what-you-need-know-driving-test

- The equilateral **triangle** pointing downwards is another special one - it's reserved for yield signs. See this shape, and you know you've got to give way.
- A **pennant** shaped sign? It's the "buzzkill" of the road, signaling no passing zones. See one, and you better stick to your lane!
- **Diamonds** are a driver's best friend. They're warning signs, typically bright yellow, alerting you to upcoming potential hazards or changes in road conditions – think sharp turns, merging lanes, or pedestrian crossings.
- The five-sided **pentagon** signs are typically associated with school zones and school crossing zones. Spot one of these, and it's time to slow down, look around for children, and ensure you're obeying school zone speed limits.
- **Round** signs have a special role - they're typically used as railroad advance warning signs. So if you come across a big yellow circle on your route, be prepared for a train crossing ahead!

There you have it! Understanding these shapes can be a lifesaver, especially in challenging driving conditions or when a sign's legibility is compromised. Remember: the shapes aren't about looking cool, but rather a critical component in conveying vital road rules.

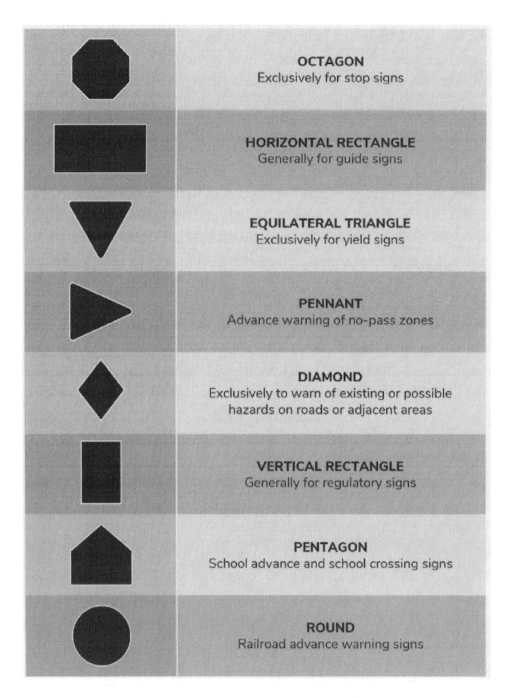

Figure 2: Traffic Sign Shapes[2]

Regulatory Signs

Regulatory signs are a super important part of road safety, so let's jump right in. These signs are meant to regulate the flow of traffic and provide drivers with rules for the road.

---

[2] https://driversed.com/trending/california-road-signs-what-you-need-know-driving-test

They're usually rectangular, but there are a few exceptions. And you might notice they come in a couple of colors - typically white and black, but you'll also see red. Below is a rundown with everything you need to know about them.

R2-4 (CA)	R3 (CA)	R6-3 (CA)	R6-3A (CA)	R6-4 (CA)	R6-4A (CA)	R13A (CA)	R13B (CA)	R18A (CA)	R18A (CA)

R18B (CA)	R20A (CA)	R20D-1 (CA) / R20D-2 (CA)	R20D-3 (CA)	R20D-4 (CA)	R20H (CA)	R20-1 (CA)	R20-1A (CA)	R21 (CA)	R22 (CA)

R23 (CA)	R24 (CA)	R25 (CA)	R26 (CA)	R26A (CA)	R26A(S) (CA)	R26B (CA)	R26C (CA)	R26F (CA)	R26J (CA)

R26(S) (CA)	R27 (CA)	R27A (CA)	R28 (CA)	R28A (CA)	R28A(S) (CA)	R28B (CA)	R28(S) (CA)	R29 (CA)	R30 (CA)

R30A (CA)	R31 (CA)	R31(S) (CA)	R32 (CA)	R32A (CA)	R32B (CA)	R33 (CA)	R33A (CA)	R33B (CA)	R33C (CA)

R36 (CA)	R37 (CA)	R38 (CA)	R38(S) (CA)	R40 (CA)	R44A (CA)	R44B (CA)	R44C (CA)	R47 (CA)	R47A (CA)

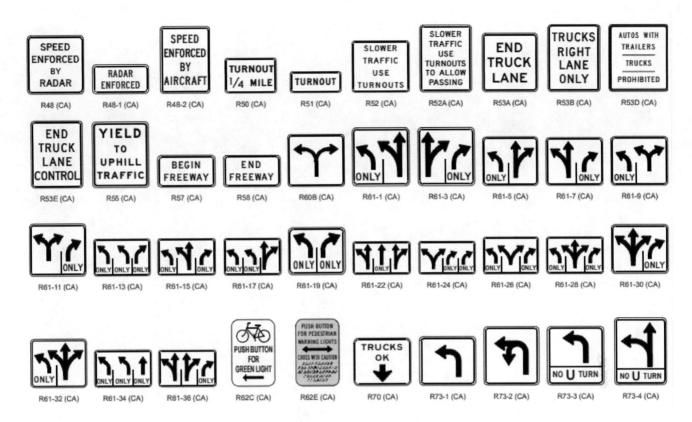

Figure 3: Examples of Federal and California Regulatory Signs[3]

Warning Signs

Let's talk about warning signs in California – the road's way of saying, "Hey, watch out, something's coming up!"

First off, warning signs in California, like in the rest of the U.S., are usually diamond-shaped and yellow, apparently this particular combo was thought to be the best to grab your attention! With no further ado, let's jump into it:

---

[3] https://www.sterndahl.com/pdf/Calif-Sign-Chart.pdf

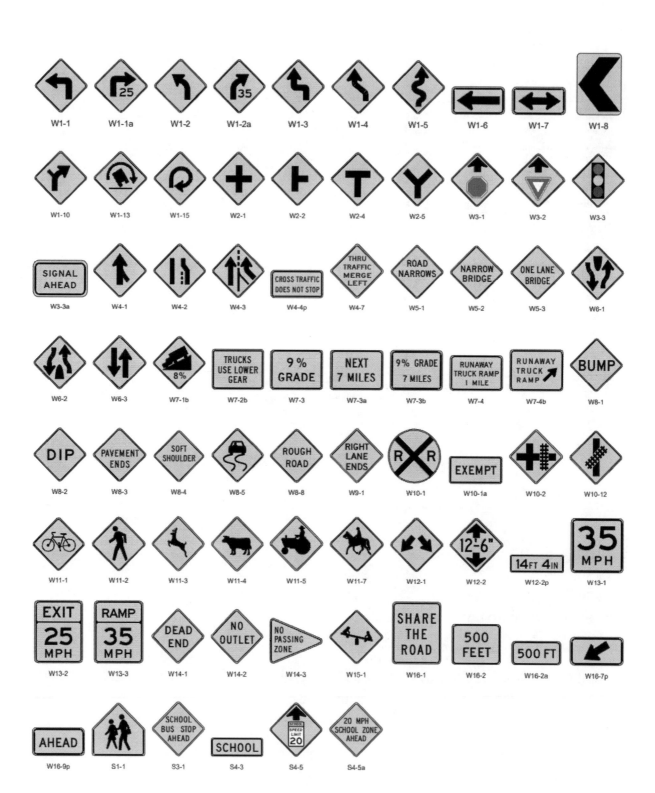

W1-1	W1-1a	W1-2	W1-2a	W1-3	W1-4	W1-5	W1-6	W1-7	W1-8
W1-10	W1-13	W1-15	W2-1	W2-2	W2-4	W2-5	W3-1	W3-2	W3-3
W3-3a	W4-1	W4-2	W4-3	W4-4p	W4-7	W5-1	W5-2	W5-3	W6-1
W6-2	W6-3	W7-1b	W7-2b	W7-3	W7-3a	W7-3b	W7-4	W7-4b	W8-1
W8-2	W8-3	W8-4	W8-5	W8-8	W9-1	W10-1	W10-1a	W10-2	W10-12
W11-1	W11-2	W11-3	W11-4	W11-5	W11-7	W12-1	W12-2	W12-2p	W13-1
W13-2	W13-3	W14-1	W14-2	W14-3	W15-1	W16-1	W16-2	W16-2a	W16-7p
W16-9p	S1-1	S3-1	S4-3	S4-5	S4-5a				

Figure 4: Examples of Federal and California Warning Signs[4]

---

[4] https://www.sterndahl.com/pdf/Calif-Sign-Chart.pdf

Guide Signs

Guide signs are the gentle road whisperers keeping you clued in and steering right as you traverse the Californian landscapes. Typically rectangular and dressed in various colors, these signs play the role of your co-pilot, ensuring you know your location, your destination, and how to get there. Given California's diverse geography, these signs are absolutely indispensable. Let's get to know them a bit better:

- First off, the **green** ones. Think of these as your compass on the road, offering directions, distances, and place names. Signs bearing messages like "Los Angeles, 60 miles" or "Exit 19B: San Francisco" would sport this color. They were Google Maps before Google Maps was even a twinkle in the internet's eye!
- **Blue** signs are next. They're like friendly concierges, pointing you towards services in the vicinity, such as gas stations, restaurants, motels, and hospitals. Spot a blue sign with a big 'H' and an arrow? You're not far from a hospital. A sign showing a knife and fork indicates food services nearby. It's the road's way of saying, "In need of a break? I've got just the spot for you."
- **Brown** signs have a special role – they're your ticket to recreational and cultural landmarks. These nudge you towards state parks, historic sites, museums, and more. In California, these signs will help you find gems like Yosemite National Park or the historic city of Monterey. They're the road's way of offering, "Had enough driving for a bit? Here's a fascinating place to explore."

Figure 5: Examples of Federal and California Guide Signs[5]

4.3 Traffic Signals

let's dive into the world of traffic signals in California. They're kind of like the conductors of the roadway orchestra, helping everyone move in harmony.

Steady Signal Lights

First, let's chat about steady signal lights, the classic trio we all know and love: red, yellow, and green.

- **Red** is like the traffic cop telling you to halt right there.
- **Yellow**, contrary to some beliefs, isn't a dare to speed up – it's a polite heads-up that the light's about to turn red, so you should prepare to stop if it's safe to do so.
- **Green,** of course, is your friendly go-ahead.

---

[5] https://www.sterndahl.com/pdf/Calif-Sign-Chart.pdf

Figure 6: Steady Signal Lights[6]

- **Red Arrow:** Hold on. Don't make the movement shown by the arrow until the green light appears. After stopping, you may turn right if there is not a NO TURN ON RED sign and the way is clear. You may turn left from a one-way street onto a one-way street that has traffic moving to the left. You must yield the right-of-way to pedestrians in the crosswalk and oncoming traffic.
- **Yellow Arrow (Steady):**
- The green arrow is ending or the light is about to turn red. Hold your horses, racer, and stop if you can safely do so.
- **Yellow Arrow (Flashing):** Turns are allowed in the direction of the arrow. The oncoming traffic has a green light, watch out!. Yield to oncoming traffic and pedestrians.
- **Green Arrow:** You may make a turn in the direction of the arrow. If the red light is illuminated at the same time, you must be in the proper lane for such a turn. You must yield the right-of-way to vehicles and pedestrians in the intersection.

---

[6] California Driver's Handbook

Figure 7: Steady Signal Lights with arrows[7]

Flashing Signal Lights

Next up, we have flashing signal lights. A flashing red light is basically a stop sign, telling you to stop and proceed only when it's safe. Meanwhile, a flashing yellow light is a bit like a cautious whisper, telling you to slow down, be alert, and proceed with care.

Lane Signals

Lane signals are interesting. They hang over lanes and give instructions specific to that lane. A green arrow means you can use the lane, while a red 'X' is the lane's way of saying "Sorry, I'm closed." A steady yellow 'X' means the lane is about to change directions, and a flashing yellow 'X' tells you the lane is only for left turns.

Ramp Signals

Ramp signals, or ramp meters, are traffic signals that control the flow of traffic onto freeways. They operate as a sort of bouncer at a nightclub, determining when cars can enter to keep traffic on the freeway flowing smoothly. A green light lets one car go, while a red light tells the others to wait their turn.

---

[7] California Driver's Handbook

Pedestrian Signals

Finally, let's talk about pedestrian signals. There are two key symbols here:

- **A steady walking person or WALK (often in white)** means it's safe for pedestrians to cross.
- **A flashing or steady DON'T WALK or 'hand' symbol (usually in orange or red)** means pedestrians should not start crossing. If the hand is flashing and you've already started crossing, continue to the other side but make it snappy. Sometimes next to the flashing hand you'll find a countdown indicating how many seconds you have left to finish crossing.
- **Diagonal Crossing:** These are crisscross and diagonal crosswalks that allow pedestrians to cross the intersection in any direction at the same time. Cross only when the WALK signal allows it.

Figure 8: Pedestrian Signals[8]

4.4 Right-of-Way Rules

Alright, let's chat about the right-of-way in California, which is basically the traffic version of "after you, no please, after you." It's all about good manners, patience, and most importantly, safety.

---

[8] California Driver's Handbook

Intersections

First off, let's talk about intersections. In California, if two drivers pull up at an intersection simultaneously, the driver on the left needs to yield to the driver on the right. It's like an unwritten rule of courtesy on the road. However, if you roll up to an intersection and a car is already there, then you should yield to that car, regardless of where it's coming from.

And when it comes to an intersection with stop signs at all four corners, it works like a polite game of "you go, no you go." The first vehicle at the intersection gets the first turn. If two vehicles reach the intersection at the same time, the driver on the left should yield to the driver on the right. Think of it as a four-way stop meet and greet, where everyone takes their turn..

Making turns

Alright, my friend, get ready as we're about to veer – yes, pun intended – into the thrilling world of California's road rules concerning turns. Be it a relaxed right or a daring left across the bustling traffic, understanding how to navigate turns correctly is essential for cruising smoothly on California's diverse streets.

Let's kick off with a right turn. If you're in the right lane and planning to take a right, the first thing you gotta do is: flash that indicator! Signaling at least 100 feet before the turn isn't just a polite gesture – it's the law, my friend. Once you've done that, make sure everything's all clear – check your mirrors, peek over your shoulder, and keep an eye out for pedestrians or cyclists. Once you're confident that it's safe, execute your turn, making sure to stay in the right lane of the road you're entering.

Now, onto a left turn: the drill is quite similar. You'll need to signal your intention well in advance of the turn and shift to the far-left lane if you're not there already. Keep your eyes peeled for any oncoming traffic, and only venture when it's clear and safe. Also, don't forget to yield to pedestrians who may be on the crosswalk. Once the coast is clear, smoothly turn into the left lane of the road you're entering.

For both right and left turns, if there are multiple turn lanes, stick to your lane during the turn. In other words, if you initiated the turn in the leftmost right-turn lane, you should end the turn in the leftmost lane of the road you're joining.

Now, a special mention about U-turns in California: they're generally allowed at intersections unless there's a sign specifically prohibiting them. But remember, safety first! You must always yield to oncoming traffic and pedestrians.

Let's also discuss red lights. In California, it's typically legal to turn right on red after making a full stop and ensuring it's safe to proceed – unless, of course, there's a sign indicating you can't. For turning left on red, it's only permissible if you're turning from a one-way street onto another one-way street, and again, only if there's no sign indicating otherwise.

And there you have it, that's the scoop on making turns in the Golden State. Just remember to always signal your intentions, stay aware of others on the road, and take your sweet time. No need to hurry – after all, we're soaking up the California vibes!

Roundabouts

Roundabouts, or as some folks refer to them, traffic circles, might seem a bit like a carousel for cars, but once you get the rhythm, they're really quite seamless. So, let's embark on a mini roundabout journey, California-style.

First things first, as you're nearing a roundabout, make sure to ease off the gas. California roundabouts typically come with speed limits hovering around 15 to 20 mph. You might also notice a yield sign, which means you'll need to give way to traffic already in the roundabout - they hold the right-of-way.

While you're holding back for your opportunity to join in, determine which exit you'll be taking from the roundabout. If you're planning a right turn or going straight, stick to the right lane. If you're going straight, executing a left turn, or contemplating a U-turn, you'll typically want to position yourself in the left lane. But always abide by the road signs and pavement markings, as rules can alter depending on the roundabout's design.

Okay, you've slowed down, you've yielded, and you know your path. Now it's time to glide into the roundabout. Just bear in mind: in the U.S., including California, roundabouts move counter-clockwise. That's to your right, my friend!

Once you're part of the roundabout, don't hit the brakes. Continue flowing with the traffic until you reach your desired exit. And stay alert for pedestrians and cyclists, as they can cross at dedicated crosswalks encircling the roundabout.

When you've made it around to your exit, flick on your right indicator to signal others that you're about to depart the roundabout. Exit at your pre-selected point, and voila, you've successfully navigated a California roundabout!

If it's your debut, roundabouts can feel somewhat like a twister. But armed with these tips, you'll be circling them like a champ in no time. Just remember, it's all about going with the flow, and of course, safety always comes first.

Pedestrians & Emergency Vehicles

Let's not overlook our foot-traveling friends. California law stipulates that drivers must yield to pedestrians lawfully crossing the street in a crosswalk, be it marked or unmarked. That's their domain, so we need to honor it.

And here's another crucial point: when emergency vehicles come zooming with their lights flashing and sirens wailing, whether they're police cruisers, fire engines, or ambulances, you must always cede the right-of-way. Pull over to the nearest edge of the roadway, and wait for them to zip past.

Provisions concerning pedestrians and emergency vehicles will be delved into more comprehensively in Chapter 7 – Sharing the Road.

And there you have it, a detailed exploration of right-of-way rules in California. Just remember, when unsure, it's always better to yield excessively than insufficiently. After all, a touch of added courtesy can contribute significantly to maintaining our roads safe..

4.5 Speed Limits

Let's shift gears and discuss speed limits in California! They might not be the most exhilarating aspect of a coastal drive along the Pacific, but they're absolutely crucial for everyone's safety on the road.

Speed limits vary across California, depending on the type of roadway and its location. However, as a general rule, these are the typical maximum speed limits you can expect:

- **Interstates and highways:** On these multi-lane, high-speed roads, the usual speed limit is 65 mph, though on some rural freeways, this could go up to 70 mph. In more congested urban areas, this might drop to 55 mph. Always be sure to keep an eye out for the posted speed limit signs.

- **Two-lane undivided highways:** On these roads, the speed limit typically hovers around 55 mph, but this can change based on the location and conditions.
- **Other state highways:** For most other state highways, the speed limit is generally 65 mph.
- **Residential and business areas:** Once you've left the open roads and entered more densely populated areas, the speed limit typically decreases to 25 mph. If it's a bustling area with a high number of pedestrians, it might be even lower.
- **School zones:** This is a biggie. In school zones when the flashers are blinking, the speed limit drops significantly, often to 25 mph. Believe me, they take this one seriously - being caught speeding in a school zone can result in a hefty fine.

Keep in mind that these are maximum speed limits under ideal conditions. If it's raining cats and dogs, or you're enveloped in a thick San Francisco fog, or the road's in poor shape, you should slow down. The posted speed limit isn't a goal; it's a limit, and sometimes it's safer to cruise below it.

California also has laws that can penalize you for driving too slowly, particularly on highways. If your turtle-paced driving disrupts the flow of traffic, it can be as hazardous as speeding.

And finally, let's not forget about California's Move Over law. If you spot an emergency vehicle with its lights flashing on the roadside, you need to either shift over a lane or, if you can't do that safely, slow down to a safer speed.

So, whether you're navigating the scenic Pacific Coast Highway, exploring the expansive Central Valley, or cruising through the vibrant streets of Los Angeles, remember to keep tabs on your speed and adhere to the legal limits. Drive safe, and savor the journey!

4.6 Passing and Overtaking

Alright, so you're cruising along one of California's highways, and you encounter a vehicle that's moving at a more leisurely pace than you'd prefer. You're ready to overtake them, but you want to ensure you're doing it correctly. Smart move, my friend! Let's break this down step by step.

Firstly, ensure it's both legal and safe to pass. If you're in a no-passing zone – usually indicated by a double solid yellow line on your side of the road – then sorry, it's a no-go, amigo.

It's also unsafe to overtake near intersections, railroad crossings, or whenever your visibility is compromised, like on a curve or the crest of a hill.

Once you've confirmed it's safe and legal to pass, check your mirrors and blind spot to verify that no one is trying to pass you. Nothing spoils an overtaking maneuver quite like discovering too late that someone else had the same idea!

Next up, signal your intention to pass by using your left turn signal. This isn't just a friendly gesture; it's a legal requirement in California. It alerts the driver you're overtaking, as well as anyone behind you, to your plans.

Now you're primed to make your move. Shift into the left lane (on a multi-lane highway) or into the oncoming traffic lane (on a two-lane road) and accelerate to overtake the slower vehicle. But don't get overzealous with that acceleration – remember, the speed limit still applies, even when passing.

As you're overtaking the vehicle, be sure to leave plenty of room before returning to your lane. A handy rule of thumb is to wait until you can see the vehicle's headlights in your rearview mirror. Then, signal your right turn and seamlessly return to your lane.

Here's an extra tip: if someone is overtaking you, it's best to maintain your speed and not make their maneuver more challenging by speeding up. If they're overtaking you, they're already going faster than you are, and your acceleration might befuddle them and potentially cause a risky situation.

So there you have it! That's your guide on how to overtake another car in California. Just remember to be patient, observant, and always signal your intentions. Safe travels!.

4.7 Parking Regulations

Let's cruise into the exciting arena of parking in California, which some people might dub as the game of securing the best spot without crossing any legal lines.

First and foremost, keep your eyes peeled for any signage that could point to parking restrictions. You know the kind: "No Parking Any Time", "Permit Parking Only". California is filled with these, especially in bustling places like Los Angeles or San Francisco, and in residential neighborhoods. Brushing off these signs can earn you a sizeable ticket.

You might be wondering, "What about when there aren't any signs?" Well, my friend, there are still a few spots where parking is a definite no-go. Let me break it down for you.

- **Intersections:** Stay clear of parking within 20 feet of an intersection. It hampers visibility for other drivers, which is a serious safety concern.
- **Fire hydrants:** Always keep at least 15 feet between your car and a fire hydrant. You never know when emergency services might need access, and you definitely don't want your car to be an obstacle.
- **Crosswalks:** Avoid parking within 20 feet of a crosswalk at an intersection. This space is crucial for pedestrians to cross safely.
- **Fire stations:** Maintain a distance of 20 feet if you're parking on the same side of the street, or 75 feet if you're on the opposite side.
- **Railroad crossings**: Keep at least 50 feet away. Trains can come barreling through faster than you'd think, and you don't want your vehicle near those tracks.
- **Bike lanes:** These are not bonus parking spaces. It might seem tempting if you see an open stretch, but parking in bike lanes is both hazardous and illegal.

Additionally, never park on sidewalks, in front of driveways, or anywhere that obstructs a curb ramp. If you're parking on the street, your car should face the direction of traffic. And in coastal areas, keep an eye out for signs about marine life – you don't want to disrupt the state's diverse ecosystem.

So there you have it, the nuts and bolts of parking in California. It might seem like a lot to remember, but don't fret – most of it boils down to common sense and being considerate of others..

4.8 School Bus and Emergency Vehicle Procedures

Let's start with school buses. California law lays it out pretty plainly: you must halt for a stationary school bus. Whether you're driving in the opposite direction or not, if that school bus has its stop sign displayed and red lights flashing, you're expected to stop. The one exception is if you're driving on a road that's divided by a physical barrier or a median; then you can proceed with caution. But if the road isn't divided, you have to stop, regardless of whether you're on the other side. Why? Well, the goal is to protect the kiddos who might be hopping on or off the bus.

Moving on to emergency vehicles - this includes police cars, fire engines, ambulances, and even tow trucks. When one is zooming your way with lights flashing and sirens wailing, California law obliges you to move to the right-hand edge of the road and stop until it's gone past. This is known as the "Move Over, Slow Down Law".

But the Move Over, Slow Down Law doesn't only kick in when an emergency vehicle is speeding towards you. It also applies when there are emergency vehicles parked on the roadside. In such cases, if you're on a road with multiple lanes in your direction, you're required to move over to a lane not adjacent to the emergency vehicle, if it's safe to do so. If you can't safely move over, or you're on a two-lane road, then you need to slow down to a safe and prudent speed.

These rules aren't just about being polite; they're about safety. School buses and emergency vehicles are carrying out critical duties, and adhering to the right procedures around them helps ensure they can perform those duties safely. Plus, it helps you dodge a hefty fine!

So next time you're zipping along California's scenic routes and you see a school bus or hear those sirens, you'll know exactly what to do. Remember, it's all about prioritizing safety!

4.9 Driving in Special Conditions (e.g., Night, Fog, Rain)

Cruising along California's roadways can be a dream, what with the jaw-dropping coastal routes and sun-drenched boulevards. But, when the weather decides to throw a curveball, it can get a little tricky. Nighttime, fog, rain – each comes with its unique set of challenges, and California, despite its Golden State reputation, experiences all of them.

Driving at night in California might seem like a straightforward affair – but there are a few pointers to remember. California is home to a vast array of wildlife, and animals like deer, raccoons, and even the occasional bear might decide to take a moonlit saunter across the road. It's a good idea to drive a bit slower after sunset, and always keep your high beams ready to flick on when needed, but don't forget to dip them for oncoming traffic.

Dealing with nighttime driving also means contending with the infamous "California fog". This can roll in surprisingly quickly, drastically reducing visibility. If you find yourself enveloped in it, remember to slow down and turn on your fog lights or low beam headlights. High beams can reflect off the fog and actually make visibility worse. And don't let familiarity breed complacency. Fog can make even well-known routes seem entirely foreign.

Next up, let's talk rain. When it rains in California, it can really come down hard, especially during the winter months. Heavy rain reduces visibility and makes the roads as slick as an ice rink. If you're caught in a downpour, slowing down is the first order of business. Maintain more distance than usual from the vehicle ahead, and use your wipers and headlights to improve visibility.

Here's a handy tip: in California, it's actually against the law to drive with your hazard lights on in the rain. Some folks think it makes them more visible, but in reality, it can confuse other drivers and create a hazard. So remember, when the wipers are on, the lights are on, but leave those hazard lights off unless you're stationary and need to warn others of a hazard.

And let's not forget about the peculiar California weather phenomenon known as "sudden downpours". These are instances where it's sunny one minute and pouring rain the next. They're unexpected but can also lead to stunning rainbows that may distract drivers, so stay vigilant!

Lastly, while California might not have a hurricane season like Florida, it does have its wildfire season, which can pose some severe driving challenges. From poor visibility due to smoke to potential road closures, it's best to avoid driving in these conditions if possible. If you have to hit the road, exercise extreme caution, and keep an eye on local news and traffic updates.

There you go. Navigating California's unique driving conditions is all about awareness, patience, and caution. It might seem daunting initially, but with care and attention, your California driving experience can remain safe and enjoyable, no matter the weather.

5 Violations, Penalties, and Procedures

5.1 Traffic Violations and Fines

Ah, traffic violations and fines — the slightly bitter part of driving. We all trip up sometimes, don't we? But, knowing the traffic laws and the repercussions of not following them in California is crucial.

Speeding: It's More About Safety... Not Speed

Alright, let's get into speeding, a widespread traffic violation that carries its fair share of penalties. The fines you could face for speeding in California may differ based on how much you're over the speed limit. It's somewhat like a rising ladder of penalties. So, let's break it down:

- If you're nabbed going just a tad over the speed limit, say **1 to 5 miles per hour**, you could be looking at fines starting around $35 to $50. Consider it a friendly nudge to watch that speedometer.
- Okay, so you're driving a bit faster and exceed the speed limit by **6 to 15 miles per hour**. In this case, the fines can escalate. You might be slapped with fines starting from $70 to $100. Yikes, that does sting a bit, huh?
- Stepping on the gas a bit more? If you're clocked going **16 to 25 miles per hour** over the limit, the fines can hike further. You could be looking at fines starting from $100 to $200. That's a more serious slap on the wrist, urging you to ease up and keep it safe.
- But, if you're really going pedal to the metal and exceed the limit **by 26 miles per hour or more**, the fines can get seriously steep. You might be hit with fines starting from $200 to $500. That's a major punch to your pocket!

Remember, these fine amounts are rough estimates and can change based on the jurisdiction and the specifics of your situation. Also, repeated offenses or speeding in sensitive zones, like school zones or construction zones, can lead to even heftier fines.

Let's not forget the ultimate goal here — ensuring safety on the roads. So, always stick to the speed limits, stay alert to those signs, and get to your destination unscathed. Happy driving, compadre!

Red Light and Stop Sign Violations: Pause and Obey

Ah, the infamous red light and stop sign violations—those cringe-worthy moments when someone barrels through an intersection or nonchalantly glides past a stop sign. It's not only perilous, but it can also pack a punch in penalties.

If you're nabbed running a red light or failing to do a full stop at a stop sign in California, you might get an unwelcome gift—a traffic ticket. Let's unpack the details:

- **Running a red light:** In California, fines for running a red light can fluctuate based on the specific jurisdiction and circumstances. You could be staring at fines starting around $238 or even higher. That smarts.
- **Stop sign violation:** Cruising past a stop sign without halting entirely? That's a massive faux pas. In California, fines for stop sign violations also depend on the jurisdiction and circumstances. You could be dealing with fines starting around $238 or more.

Bear in mind these fines are rough guesstimates and can change depending on the specific jurisdiction where the infraction occurred. Moreover, repeated violations can result in elevated fines, and racking up too many points on your driving record can lead to other repercussions, like license suspension.

Let's face it—paying fines isn't a joyride. But the real deal behind these fines is to instill safe driving practices and discourage hazardous conduct on the road. It's all about safeguarding everyone—motorists, pedestrians, and cyclists alike.

So, when you roll up to a red light or a stop sign, take a pause, respect the traffic laws, and make that full stop. Let's make our roads safer, one intersection at a time.

Reckless Driving: Easy There, Road Warrior

Reckless driving—it's like the Bigfoot of traffic violations. We've all witnessed those daredevil drivers with an apparent appetite for speed or penchant for perilous moves on the road. Reckless driving isn't child's play.

Picture this: you're sailing smoothly, and suddenly, you spy a driver who's darting between lanes, tailgating, or executing other hazardous stunts. That's a classic case of reckless driving, my friend. In California, the fallout for this type of behavior can be quite substantial.

Now, for the nitty-gritty—the fines. If you're caught indulging in reckless driving in the Golden State, you might end up shouldering some serious penalties. The fines for reckless driving can differ based on the specifics and jurisdiction, but you could be hit with fines starting around $145 to $1,000. Yikes, that's a real pinch!

But hold your horses! Reckless driving in California isn't just about the fines. It can also lead to other fallouts, such as soaring insurance rates, points on your driving record, and even potential criminal charges. So, it's safe to say reckless driving is a grave offense that should be dodged like the plague.

Remember, these fines aren't about lining coffers—they're to discourage recklessness and encourage safe driving habits. The aim is to secure the safety of everyone on the road, yourself, and fellow asphalt comrades included.

So, let's pledge to drive prudently, abide by the traffic laws, and stay mindful of our actions behind the wheel. Reckless driving isn't worth the gamble—it's not only risky but can also bear long-lasting repercussions. Let's keep our California roads secure for all.

Seat Belt and Child Restraint Violations: Strap In, Stay Secure

We've already stressed the significance of strapping in and ensuring our tiny tots' safety in the car. Now, let's view the issue from another angle: the fallout for those who disregard the rules.

In California, seat belt and child restraint violations aren't taken lightly, and they pack some serious consequences. If you're nabbed in California without your seat belt, you might be looking at a fine. But here's the real kicker—it's not just about the dough, it's fundamentally about our wellbeing and that of our passengers. So, let's make it second nature to always buckle up, whether we're steering the wheel or along for the ride.

Now, let's talk about our small fries—our treasured cargo. When it comes to child restraint violations, it's imperative to provide the correct safety measures for our kids on the road. In California, child restraint violations can also result in fines. The specifics can fluctuate based on the situation, but they're enforced to underline the crucial role of securing our children in suitable child safety seats or restraints relative to their age and size.

Keep in mind, these fines are not just about the monetary hit—they're about safeguarding our cherished ones. Properly strapping in our children is a key step in their safety during car journeys. So, let's ensure we're using the right child safety seats or restraints for their age and size, and always make a double-take that everything is fastened securely.

When it comes to seat belt and child restraint violations, the aim is to nurture a culture of safety on our roads. So, let's be diligent drivers and passengers, strap ourselves in, and guarantee our little ones are properly restrained. Together, we can pave the way for a safer driving environment for all.

Texting and Driving: Hold That Thought

Texting and driving is the pinnacle of distractions when you're in control of a vehicle. We've covered this before, but I want to underscore the legal implications. In fact, in California, texting and driving isn't just hazardous—it's also illegal.

Imagine this: you're coasting down the highway, and all of a sudden, your phone emits that familiar "ping". It's tempting to grab it, but hang on! In California, it's against the law to text while at the wheel. Law enforcement doesn't take this violation lightly, and for good reason—it's a significant distraction that puts everyone on the roadway in danger.

If you're nabbed texting and driving in the Golden State, you might be looking at a fine. Now, let's delve into the specifics: the fine for texting and driving can vary based on the circumstances and jurisdiction.

So, here's the lowdown: when you're steering that wheel, keep your phone out of reach. It can wait! It's all about keeping your eyes on the prize—driving safely and attentively. That text or social media scroll can hold off until you're safely parked or have arrived at your destination.

5.2 Points System

It's kind of like a scoreboard keeping tabs on our road habits. The concept is simple—drive properly, and you're golden, slip up, and those points start piling up. Let's break it down:

Think of it as a game where every time you violate a traffic rule or get a citation, you rack up points. In California, it's a similar deal with your driver's license. The points system is a way to monitor your on-road behavior and ensure everyone behind the wheel is held accountable for their actions.

Here's the rundown: when you commit certain traffic offenses, you'll pile up points on your license. These points fluctuate depending on the severity of the violation. For example, a ticket for speeding might add a point, while a more serious violation like reckless driving can saddle you with a larger number of points.

Now, you might be thinking, "Why should I bother about these points?" Well, here's the scoop—accumulating too many points can lead to repercussions. If you gather too many points within a specific timeframe, your license could be suspended. And that's not a situation anyone wants, right? Below you can find the exact number of points and the timeframes that can result in a license suspension:

- **4 points within 12 months - 30-day suspension**
- **6 points within 24 months - Six-month suspension**
- **8 points within 36 months - One-year suspension**

So, the trick is to drive sensibly, adhere to the road rules, and steer clear of those traffic offenses that add points to your record. It's all about making prudent choices behind the wheel and considering the consequences of our actions.

But hey, it's not all dire warnings. On a positive note, if you drive cautiously and maintain a clean slate without accumulating any points, that's a big thumbs up! It shows you're a mindful driver who puts safety first.

Now, if you do find yourself racking up points, don't panic! It's not the end of the road. Points do expire, and they can be reduced or removed if you complete certain driving courses or keep a clean record for a set period.

Here's the takeaway: let's aim to be considerate drivers and keep our licenses point-free. It's all about acknowledging our responsibilities on the road, abiding by traffic laws, and prioritizing our own safety as well as others'.

So, let's strive for a perfect score—a spotless driving record with zero points. By doing so, we'll contribute to safer California roads and enjoy a stress-free driving experience.

5.3 DUI Laws and Penalties

We all know the importance of driving sober, but sometimes people make poor choices. In California, DUI, or driving under the influence, is a big deal and comes with some hefty penalties. So, let's dive deep into this.

Imagine this: you're out enjoying yourself with friends, maybe you've had a couple of drinks. The idea of driving home might seem okay, but hold on a second! Driving under the influence is not only risky but also against the law. In California, the law takes a hard stand against DUI, handing out severe penalties to discourage people from such dangerous actions.

Now, about those penalties. Remember, they can vary based on the situation and whether it's your first rodeo or you're a repeat offender. Here's a general rundown:

- **License Suspension:** If you're hit with a DUI conviction in California, say goodbye to your driver's license for a while. For a first offense, this could mean a suspension for six months. Got more than one offense? Expect a longer suspension.
- **Fines:** The fines for DUI in California are nothing to sneeze at. For a first offense, you're looking at fines from $390 to $1,000, plus additional penalty assessments. For repeat offenders, the fines can get steeper.
- **Probation:** Aside from your wallet getting lighter and license suspension, DUI offenders might find themselves on probation. This means you've got to follow certain rules, like attending DUI education programs, doing some community service, or getting substance abuse counseling.
- **Ignition Interlock Device (IID):** Depending on your case, you might have to install an IID in your car. This gizmo checks your blood alcohol concentration (BAC) and won't let your car start if it sniffs out alcohol.
- **Jail Time:** For serious DUI offenses, you could end up behind bars. How long you'll be wearing orange depends on your specific case and if you're a repeat offender.

Keep in mind that these penalties can change, and repeat offenses usually mean harsher penalties. Also, a DUI conviction can leave a lasting scar on your insurance rates and overall driving record.

But here's the thing—we should always put safety first, both ours and others', by staying sober behind the wheel. It's never worth the risk or the potential consequences that come with a DUI conviction. So, let's be smart, folks. If we've had a few drinks, let's call a cab, use a rideshare service, or public transportation. It's as simple as that.

5.4 Dealing with Accidents

Navigating through accidents can indeed be a rollercoaster of emotions and stress. We wish it never comes down to this, but if you do find yourself in an accident in California, it's vital to know the next steps. Let's break it down the California way:

Picture this: you're out driving, minding your own business, and out of the blue, CRASH! An accident happens. It's a nerve-wracking moment, but hang in there—we'll guide you through the process.

Firstly, take a moment to calm your nerves. It's normal to feel flustered, but doing your best to stay collected will help. Here's your game plan:

- **Safety Comes First**: Do a quick check on yourself and others for injuries. If anyone is hurt and needs immediate medical help, dial 911 straight away. Remember, safety is the priority!
- **Secure the Scene:** If it's possible and safe, and your vehicles aren't totaled, shift them to the roadside or a secure spot. This helps avoid further mishaps and lets traffic move without obstruction.
- **Swap Info:** Next, gather and exchange information. Share and get contact and insurance details with the other driver(s) involved in the accident. This should include their name, contact number, insurance provider, and policy number. If there are witnesses, getting their details would be helpful too.
- **Document Everything:** Snap photos of the accident scene, capturing the damages to vehicles and visible injuries if any. These can be instrumental when it comes to insurance claims or any potential legal issues.
- **Report the Accident:** In California, if the accident involves injuries, death, or property damage exceeding $750, you need to report it to the California Department of Motor Vehicles within ten days. You might also need to inform local police or California Highway Patrol right after the incident.
- **Reach Out to Your Insurer:** Get in touch with your insurance provider at the earliest to report the accident. They will guide you through their claim process and tell you the next steps.

Remember, maintaining a cool head and cooperation is key when handling accidents. Refrain from accepting blame or making any speculative statements about the event. Let the police and insurance folks decide who's at fault based on evidence and statements given.

Handling accidents can be a daunting task, but following these steps can make the process more manageable. Remember, the well-being and safety of everyone involved is what matters the most. Ensure everyone's okay and gets the necessary medical help if required.

Times like these call for support from loved ones, legal experts, or insurance reps who can help you navigate the post-accident landscape. Stay calm, follow the necessary steps, and remember that accidents happen—it's how we deal with them that counts.

5.5 License Suspension, Cancellation, and Revocation

License suspension, cancellation, and revocation—the stuff of nightmares for any driver. We all hope never to land in a situation where our driving rights are pulled from under us. But in California, there are certain circumstances where this can indeed happen. Let's unravel the details.

Imagine this: you're cruising down the Californian roads, basking in the freedom that driving offers. Yet, unforeseen turns of life can sometimes throw a wrench in the works, endangering our driving privileges. In California, there exist scenarios that can result in license suspension, cancellation, or revocation. Let's break down each of these:

- **License Suspension:** Think of this as a temporary pause on driving. It implies that your license is momentarily nullified for a certain period. In California, reasons for license suspension can range from accumulating excessive points on your driving record, specific traffic offenses, failure to pay fines or child support, to certain medical conditions. The duration of the suspension hinges on the specific circumstances.
- **License Cancellation:** This equates to your license being completely annulled. Your driving privileges are discontinued, and you'll have to apply for a new license when you're eligible. In California, license cancellation can occur if you provide false information on your license application, if you're found ineligible for a driver's license, or if your license was mistakenly issued.

- **License Revocation**: This is akin to a long-term or permanent removal of your driving rights. Your license is revoked, and reinstating it usually involves a rigorous process. In California, license revocation can result from severe offenses such as DUI convictions, multiple traffic offenses, or certain criminal convictions.

It's crucial to bear in mind that the exact reasons leading to license suspension, cancellation, or revocation can vary, and so can the duration or the prerequisites for reinstatement. It's always a wise move to consult the California Department of Motor Vehicles (DMV) or seek legal counsel for precise and updated information regarding your particular situation.

Here's the silver lining—license suspension, cancellation, or revocation doesn't mark the end of your driving journey. There are usually measures you can take to address the issue and work towards reinstating your driving privileges. It may entail meeting certain requirements, completing driver improvement courses, or adhering to specific conditions set by the authorities.

5.6 Traffic Courts and Procedures

So, you find yourself with a traffic violation—feels like you've entered uncharted territory, right? It can be somewhat daunting, but fret not—I'm here to guide you through the process.

Picture this: you spot a traffic ticket in your mailbox or find yourself being pulled over by an officer. Not exactly the highlight of your day, but it's crucial to know how to handle the traffic court system in California. Here's the rundown:

- **Traffic Ticket:** When you get a traffic ticket, it typically details the violation, the fine amount, and the deadline by which you must respond. It's critical to go through the ticket carefully and grasp the charges you're facing.
- **Options for Responding:** In California, you generally have three choices when it comes to responding to a traffic ticket: fork over the fine, opt for a traffic school (if you're eligible), or fight the ticket in court. The decision will depend on your unique situation and your preference.
- **Paying the Fine:** If you decide to pay the fine, you can usually do it online, by mail, or in person. Make sure to do so before the deadline to dodge any extra penalties or fallout.

- **Traffic School**: Sometimes, you might be eligible to attend a traffic school to dodge points on your driving record or potential insurance rate hikes. If this option is open to you, it's a chance to brush up on your driving skills.
- **Contesting the Ticket:** If you believe you're not guilty of the violation, or you've got a legit defense, you can choose to challenge the ticket in court. This process involves standing before a judge and making your case. It's important to gather evidence, like witnesses, photographs, or any other relevant documentation to back up your defense.
- **Traffic Court Appearance**: If you opt to fight the ticket, you'll need to show up in traffic court on the assigned date. Dress appropriately and remember to be respectful in the courtroom. Lay out your case in a calm and clear manner, and heed any instructions provided by the judge.
- **Judgment and Potential Consequences:** After hearing both sides, the judge will pass a judgment regarding the ticket. If you're found guilty, you might be required to pay fines, deal with points on your driving record, attend traffic school, or other potential consequences depending on the specific violation and circumstances.

Keep in mind, traffic court procedures can slightly differ depending on the jurisdiction and your specific situation. It's always smart to consult the specific county's traffic court website or seek legal advice for accurate information related to your case.

6 California's Vehicle Requirements

6.1 Vehicle Registration

Vehicle registration—it's one of those inevitable tasks that come with car ownership. But worry not! While it might seem a bit tedious, getting your vehicle registered in California isn't really as daunting as it might seem. Let's talk about it, shall we?

Initial Vehicle Registration

Picture this: you've got that fresh-from-the-dealership or gently-used new-to-you car, or perhaps you've recently moved to California with your vehicle from another state. In both cases, you'll need to get your ride registered with the local authorities. Here's how you do it:

- First things first, gather your necessary documents: your vehicle's title, proof of California auto insurance, and your driver's license.

- Next, head on over to your local California Department of Motor Vehicles (DMV) office, or make life easier by opting for their online services if available. They'll help guide you through filling out the right forms and explain the process to you.

- Remember to bring your wallet because you'll have to pay the registration fee. This cost is based on your vehicle's value, its type, weight, and other factors. To avoid surprises, it might be a good idea to check the DMV's website for the current fee schedule before heading over.

- Once you've jumped through all the hoops, filled out your forms, and paid your fee, you'll be handed your shiny new license plate and registration documents.

Vehicle Registration Renewal

It seems like time accelerates when you have deadlines, doesn't it? Suddenly, your vehicle's registration is up for renewal. So, here's what you need to do to keep everything in order:

- Keep track of your vehicle registration's expiration date. In California, vehicle registrations typically expire on a yearly basis, so be sure to make a note of that date.

- When that time of year rolls around again, you have some options on how to renew. You can choose the convenience of online renewal through the California DMV's website, you can visit your local DMV office, or you can use the mail-in renewal service if you prefer.

- Make sure you have your current registration documents and proof of insurance on hand when you're ready to renew.

- Don't forget to budget for the renewal fee, which varies based on your vehicle's value and other factors. Check the DMV's website for the current fee structure to keep yourself updated.

- After you've navigated the renewal process and paid the necessary fees, you'll receive your new registration documents and a sticker for your license plate.

Remember, it's always crucial to keep your vehicle registration up-to-date to avoid any legal hiccups or unnecessary fines. California is pretty strict about vehicle registration rules!

So, whether you're getting your vehicle registered for the first time or you're handling the annual renewal, remember: it's all just a process. Gather your documents, pay your fees, and before you know it, you'll be back on the road, cruising down those California highways with peace of mind!

6.2 Vehicle Insurance Requirements

Vehicle insurance necessities—those unavoidable bits we have to handle as drivers. In California, just like in many states, having the correct vehicle insurance is non-negotiable. It's about keeping you and your fellow drivers safe on the roads. Let's dive into it:

Liability Insurance: Your Safeguard for Others

In sunny California, the state mandates drivers to have liability insurance. This kind of insurance covers costs if you're responsible for an accident, and someone else gets hurt or their property is damaged. It's a safety net for others on the road. So, as a Californian, you need to maintain the minimum liability insurance coverage as required by law.

Minimum Liability Coverage Specifics

Time to understand the specifics of minimum liability coverage in California:

- **$15,000 for injury or death to one person** (another driver, passenger, pedestrian, etc.): This coverage helps pay for medical and related costs if you're at fault in an accident.
- **$30,000 for injury or death to more than one person:** This coverage offers added protection if multiple people are injured or killed in an accident for which you're responsible.
- **$5,000 for property damage:** This coverage helps pay for damages you cause to someone else's property, like their car, a mailbox, or a fence.

Bear in mind, these are only the minimum requirements. You might think about higher coverage limits or additional types of coverage for more protection.

Other Coverage Types

While liability insurance is a legal obligation, you might consider other types of coverage for more comprehensive protection. These could include:

- **Uninsured Motorist Coverage:** This covers your expenses if you're in an accident caused by a driver who lacks insurance or doesn't have enough coverage.
- **Collision Coverage:** This pays for damages to your vehicle if you're in an accident, regardless of who's at fault.
- **Comprehensive Coverage:** This takes care of damages to your vehicle from events like theft, vandalism, or Mother Nature's surprises.

Look Around and Compare

When it comes to insurance, shopping around and comparing quotes from various insurance companies is always wise. Prices and coverage options differ, so it's worth spending some time finding the best match for your needs and wallet.

Having the right vehicle insurance in California isn't only a legal obligation; it's about ensuring protection for you and everyone else on the road. So, keep the minimum liability coverage, consider additional coverage options, and find the insurance that suits you best.

6.3 Safety and Emission Inspections

Safety and emissions inspections—two important things to keep our vehicles in tip-top shape and help protect the environment. In California, we want to ensure our cars are safe and environmentally friendly. Let's have a chat about these inspections:

Safety Inspections: Ensuring Safe Travels

Safety inspections are all about checking if your vehicle meets safety norms. It's about your safety, the safety of your passengers, and the safety of others on the road. The thing is—in California, safety inspections aren't usually necessary for most vehicles. So, no rush to schedule a separate safety inspection. However, regular maintenance and inspection of your vehicle to ensure it's road-ready is still crucial.

Emissions Inspections: Protecting the Environment

Now, let's switch gears to smog checks. These inspections emphasize our vehicles' environmental impact and the pollutants they emit. However, in California, it's not all cars and all the time. Smog checks are mandatory for most vehicles every two years or when the vehicle changes ownership. The goal? To keep our Golden State air clean. So, remember to have your car undergo a smog check when due, for a greener California.

Other Vehicle Inspections

Even though safety inspections aren't typically required in California, it's key to keep up with regular vehicle maintenance. Regularly check your tires, brakes, lights, and fluid levels. This routine can keep your vehicle running smoothly and help avoid any unwelcome surprises on the road.

Stay Informed and Compliant

Stay informed about any changes to California's inspection requirements. Laws evolve, so keep an eye on the California Department of Motor Vehicles (DMV) website or get in touch directly for the latest details.

Even if safety inspections aren't generally mandatory in California, the safety and upkeep of your vehicle should still be a priority. Regular checks and maintenance ensure safer roads and contribute to a healthier environment. So, stay vigilant, look after your vehicle, and relish your Californian driving escapades!

6.4 Vehicle Equipment Standards

Now onto vehicle equipment standards in California. We all desire safe vehicles, right? This is where vehicle equipment standards come into the picture. These standards make sure our cars are fitted with necessary safety-enhancing features. Let's dig into it:

Headlights and Taillights: Illuminating the Way

In the dark or in low visibility conditions, headlights and taillights are invaluable. In California, law mandates having working headlights and taillights. Make sure your headlights are functioning and correctly aimed, and use them when required. And don't neglect those taillights—they allow other drivers to spot you from behind.

Turn Signals: Signaling Your Intentions

Since we're not mind-readers, turn signals are vital—they inform other drivers when we intend to turn or change lanes. In California, it's a legal requirement to have functional turn signals. So, use them to indicate your intentions on the road. It's a small action that can greatly enhance safe driving.

Mirrors: Keeping an Eye on Things

Who doesn't appreciate a good rearview mirror? They're like a magic window to monitor what's happening behind us. In California, having at least one functional rearview mirror is a legal requirement. But why stop at one? Side mirrors extend your field of vision and are equally important. So, keep those mirrors adjusted properly to decrease blind spots and raise your road awareness.

Windshield Wipers: Rain or Shine

California has its fair share of rain, right? That's when windshield wipers save the day. It's essential to have properly functioning windshield wipers for clear visibility during rain or other adverse weather. If your wipers start streaking or leaving behind residues, it's probably time to switch them out.

Tires: The Rubber that Hits the Road

In California, it's vital to have tires with enough tread depth to ensure appropriate traction on the road. Bald or worn-out tires can affect your ability to stop or steer safely, especially in wet conditions. So, regularly inspect your tires' tread depth and replace them when needed to maintain optimal grip.

These are just a handful of examples of vehicle equipment standards in California. Familiarize yourself with all the requirements outlined by the California Department of Motor Vehicles (DMV). Regularly check your vehicle's equipment, fix any issues promptly, and prioritize safety on the road.

7 Special Driving Situations

This chapter is a special one. It's the one I thoroughly enjoyed writing, and I'm excited for you to dive in. So, get comfortable as we're about to delve into various unique driving scenarios you'll encounter on California's roads.

7.1 Highway Driving

Freeway driving...it's where the real test of driving skills comes into play, wouldn't you agree? The continuous stretches, the pace, the flow—it's all part of the quintessential American driving experience. But it comes with its unique rules and challenges, especially here in California, home to some of the busiest and longest freeways in the nation.

Enter and Exit Safely

The first major challenge with freeway driving is getting on and off the freeway. We've got on-ramps and off-ramps that demand careful navigation. Remember to use your turn signals when entering and exiting the freeway. As you're entering, aim to match your speed with the freeway traffic. This helps you to merge seamlessly without disrupting the flow of traffic.

Keep Right Except to Pass

This rule is essential. The left lane on the freeway is primarily for overtaking. If you're not passing another vehicle, stay in the middle or right lanes. This helps maintain the traffic flow and contributes to a smoother, safer ride for everyone.

Follow the Speed Limit

While the long, open stretches may tempt you to accelerate, speed limits are there for good reason. Watch out for those speed limit signs and abide by them. It's safer, and you'll avoid the risk of a speeding ticket.

Watch for Big Rigs

California's freeways are frequently occupied by semi-trucks and big rigs. Keep in mind, these vehicles have larger blind spots, take longer to stop, and may make wide turns. Give them plenty of room and always pass them on the left side, where the truck driver has better visibility.

Be Aware of HOV Lanes

Carpool lanes, or High Occupancy Vehicle (HOV) lanes, are reserved for vehicles with multiple occupants to encourage carpooling and reduce traffic congestion. If you have a passenger or two, you can use the carpool lane and avoid regular traffic. It's like a secret passage during peak hours! However, remember, you need to have the minimum number of people in your vehicle to use these lanes, usually two or more.

Stay Alert

Freeway driving, particularly on long journeys, can become monotonous and lead to fatigue. Take regular breaks, share driving responsibilities if possible, and ensure you're well-rested before hitting the road.

Follow these guidelines and it will be a smooth experience. It all boils down to staying vigilant, adhering to the rules, and being considerate of other drivers. So, get on the road, savor the drive, and remember, safety first!

7.2 City Driving

Ah, city driving! It's a totally different experience compared to the freeway driving, isn't it? With stoplights at every corner, pedestrians, cyclists, and that one driver who can't pick a lane, city driving can feel like a labyrinth at times, especially in some of our bustling California cities. But, fear not, I've got some handy tips to help you master the art of city driving.

Mind the Speed Limit

Unlike freeways, city streets have lower and frequently changing speed limits. School zones, residential neighborhoods, and downtown streets - each has its own speed limit, typically well-displayed with signs. So be vigilant and look out for those signs and follow them. It's safer and helps keep those pesky speeding tickets at bay!

Be Pedestrian Aware

In the city, you'll come across a lot more pedestrians. They might cross at intersections, mid-block, or suddenly emerge from between parked cars. And keep in mind, in

California, pedestrians have the right of way at both marked crosswalks and intersections. So stay sharp and be ready to yield.

Watch for Cyclists

California is home to a burgeoning cyclist population. This means you need to routinely check your mirrors and blind spots, particularly before turning or changing lanes. And give cyclists a wide berth when you overtake them—it's not just polite, it's required by law.

Parking Perfection

Oh, city parking, the archenemy of many drivers! Between parallel parking, multi-story parking structures, and metered parking—it can be a challenge. Take it easy, especially with parallel parking. No one nails it on the first try. And keep a watchful eye for any parking restrictions to avoid surprises. You wouldn't want a parking ticket or, worse, finding your car towed!

Expect the Unexpected

City driving can be full of surprises—a driver may brake abruptly, a pedestrian might jaywalk, or a car door might swing open unexpectedly. The key is to stay alert, maintain a safe distance from the vehicle ahead, and always be ready to react.

Remember, city driving is not a race, it's about staying safe and reaching your destination while sharing the road with a multitude of other road users. Be patient, stay alert, and don't rush. With a bit of practice, you'll be smoothly navigating through those California city streets.

7.3 Rural Driving

You know, some might not think about it, but California is more than just bustling cities and scenic coastlines—it's also home to a wealth of rural areas—vineyards, small towns, open spaces—and driving in these areas comes with its own unique set of rules and challenges. So, let's delve into it, shall we?

Watch Your Speed

Just because you're driving through the countryside doesn't mean speed limits become irrelevant. In fact, rural roads can be unpredictable with sudden bends, variable road conditions, or unforeseen obstacles. So keep tabs on your speed, and stay alert for speed limit signs.

Stay Alert for Wildlife

One of the notable aspects of rural driving in California? Wildlife. It's surprising how often deer, raccoons, or even the occasional mountain lion can appear on the road, particularly around dawn and dusk. If an animal suddenly appears in your path, brake firmly but refrain from swerving—you could end up in a ditch or in the path of oncoming traffic. I'll elaborate more on this later in the book.

Be Ready for Farm Equipment

In rural areas, it's not uncommon to find yourself sharing the road with tractors or other farm equipment. These vehicles move slowly, so patience is key. Only overtake when you have ample space and a clear view of the road ahead.

Dealing with Dirt and Gravel Roads

In the countryside, not all roads are paved. When driving on dirt or gravel, reduce your speed compared to what you'd maintain on asphalt, and maintain a safe distance from other vehicles to avoid dust and flying pebbles. Keep in mind, it's much easier to lose control, especially around bends, so exercise caution.

Keep an Eye Out for Hidden Intersections

Out in the country, not all intersections are marked with stop signs or lights, and some can be concealed by vegetation or curves in the road. Always reduce speed when approaching intersections, and stay alert for other vehicles.

Driving in rural California has its own allure—the open roads, the wildlife, the tranquility. But it also demands a distinct set of driving skills. So remember, take your time, stay vigilant, and savor the journey. Who knows, you might just discover that rural driving is your new passion!

7.4 Construction Zones

Ah, construction zones. We've all experienced it, haven't we? You're smoothly driving along, and then suddenly, you're surrounded by orange cones, lanes become narrower, and speed limits decrease. It can be a bit of a headache, particularly if you're pressed for time. But hey, it's all part of progress! These zones are where our roads and infrastructure get the much-needed upgrades to keep us moving efficiently. So, let's learn how to maneuver these areas safely here in the Golden State.

Slow Down

Speed limit signs in construction zones aren't mere suggestions—they're the law. Plus, fines often double in these areas. So slow down, not just for the sake of your wallet, but for everyone's safety.

Be Alert

Changes can occur quickly in construction zones—lane shifts, detours, workers, or equipment entering the roadway. Stay sharp and be ready to respond. Remember, the road workers are out there performing a difficult job. Let's make sure everyone gets home safe.

Keep Your Distance

Tailgating is never a good idea, particularly in construction zones. Unanticipated stops are frequent, so keep a safe distance from the vehicle in front of you to prevent any fender benders.

Obey Road Crew Flaggers and Signs

Road crew flaggers are the orchestrators of the construction ballet. They're on top of things and will help guide you safely through the chaos. So heed their directions and pay attention to all signs and work zone indicators.

Stay Calm and Patient

I get it, I really do. Construction zones can delay your trip and disrupt your meticulously planned schedule. But growing stressed or angry won't get you through any quicker. Take a deep breath, cue up some soothing tunes, and remember this is just a short-term inconvenience for long-term improvement.

Don't Forget the Night Workers

Many construction projects operate through the night when traffic is less dense. However, decreased visibility can make these zones more hazardous. So switch on your low beams when you see workers or vehicles ahead, and exercise extra caution.

Construction zones are a part of life for all of us California drivers. But with a bit of patience, caution, and respect for those improving our roads, we can navigate them safely and without much fuss. Wishing you happy (and safe) driving!

7.5 Railroad Crossings

Railroad crossings, eh? They might seem a bit vintage in our era of freeways and expressways, but they're a crucial part of our transportation system. This is especially true here in California, where we have a pretty comprehensive rail network. So, let's dive into how to approach these crossings safely:

Look, Listen, and Slow Down

This may sound reminiscent of your kindergarten years, right? But it's sound advice when it comes to railroad crossings. As you approach a crossing, reduce your speed, look in both directions, and listen. Can you hear or see a train approaching? Are the warning lights blinking? Even if the signals aren't active, pause for a moment to ensure it's safe to proceed.

Never Try to Beat a Train

This one is crucial. You'd be surprised how many folks believe they can beat a train. Spoiler alert: you can't. Trains move much quicker than they appear to, and they can't stop on a dime. If the lights are flashing or the gates are lowering, stop. No destination is worth jeopardizing your life.

Stuck on the Tracks? Get Out and Get Away

It seems like a scene straight out of a thriller: a car is stranded on the tracks with a train hurtling towards it. But it can happen. If you're stuck, exit your car, retreat from the tracks, and dial 911. If a train is imminent, run in the direction of the oncoming train but away from the tracks at a 45-degree angle to dodge any debris if the train collides with your car.

Respect the Gates and Lights

Those gates and flashing lights serve a vital purpose: your safety. Never bypass lowered gates or disregard flashing lights. It's not just illegal—it's incredibly risky.

Be Extra Cautious in Bad Weather

During heavy rain, fog, or at night, it can be harder to spot and hear an oncoming train. Exercise additional caution at railroad crossings during these times.

Railroad crossings might seem like a minor interruption in your journey, but they warrant your undivided attention. With a touch of care and caution, they're straightforward to navigate. So remember, keep your eyes and ears open, slow down, and stay safe on the roads!

7.6 Parallel Parking and Parking on Hills

Let's now address two specific parking situations: parallel parking and parking on hills.

Parallel Parking

Parallel parking is a bit of an art, but don't worry, with a little practice, you'll be able to fit into those tight city spaces in no time. Here's the step-by-step:

- Find a space that's at least one and a half times the length of your car.
- Signal right to let other drivers know you're planning to park.
- Pull up next to the car in front of the space, keeping about 2-3 feet between your cars.
- Look over your right shoulder and start backing up slowly. As your front door passes the back bumper of the car next to you, turn your wheel sharply to the right.
- Once your car is at about a 45-degree angle, straighten your wheel and continue backing in.
- When your front door aligns with the back bumper of the car next to you again, turn your wheel sharply to the left.

- Back in slowly until your car is parallel and centered in the space. Your wheels should be no more than 12 inches from the curb.
- Adjust your position if necessary, then put your car in park, engage the parking brake, and you're done!

Parking on Hills

Parking on hills has its own set of rules. You'll want to turn your wheels to prevent your car from rolling into traffic if your brakes fail:

- If you're parking uphill with a curb, turn your wheels away from the curb (to the left). When you let off the brakes, your car should roll back and the front right tire should rest against the curb.
- If you're parking downhill with a curb, turn your wheels toward the curb (to the right). When you let off the brakes, your car should roll forward and the front right tire should rest against the curb.
- If there's no curb, whether you're parking uphill or downhill, turn your wheels to the right. That way, if your car rolls, it'll go off the road, not into traffic.

One last thing: don't forget to set your parking brake, especially when parking on hills. Even with your car in park, there's still a risk of it rolling.

With these tips, you should be able to park like a pro in any situation. Just remember to always check for signs and other restrictions before you leave your car.

8 Sharing the Road

In this chapter, we're going to guide you through the nuances of sharing the road in the Golden State. From the buzzing city streets to the more peaceful suburban roads, we'll delve into the dynamics of engaging with fellow road users, embracing California's diverse driving culture, and ensuring safety amidst the constant activity.

8.1 Pedestrians

Picture this: you're cruising along a lively California street, and out of nowhere, a pedestrian appears at a crosswalk. It's crucial to remain conscious of these walkers and adopt measures to safeguard their well-being. Here's what you need to remember:

- **Respect Crosswalks and Pedestrian Right-of-Way:** Pedestrians have the right-of-way at both marked and unmarked crosswalks in California. As you approach a crosswalk, ease off the gas and be ready to stop. Yield to pedestrians crossing or about to enter the crosswalk, allowing them to cross the road safely.
- **Stay Vigilant and Survey Your Environment:** Pedestrians can be unpredictable, so it's essential to remain alert and continually scan your surroundings. Watch for pedestrians on sidewalks, near intersections, and in parking lots. Be particularly cautious during low-light conditions when visibility can be compromised.
- **Be Extra Careful in School Zones and School Crossings:** Use extra caution in school zones and around school crossings. Kids can be harder to spot and may dart into the road unexpectedly. Reduce your speed, be patient, and keep an eye out for crossing guards or school zone signs signaling reduced speed limits.
- **Avoid Distracted Driving:** Maintain your focus solely on the road and steer clear of distractions while driving. Activities like texting, using your phone, eating, and so forth can distract you and increase the risk of failing to notice pedestrians. Stay alert and put pedestrian safety first.
- **Adhere to Speed Limits and Adjust for Conditions:** Stick to the posted speed limits, especially in residential areas and zones with heavy pedestrian traffic. Adjust your speed based on road conditions, weather, and visibility. Slower speeds grant more reaction time in case a pedestrian unexpectedly steps into your path.
- **Pay Attention to Bus Stops and Transit Areas**: Bus stops and transit areas are often bustling with pedestrians. Exercise caution when passing these spots and be ready for people getting on or off buses. Allow buses extra space and stay aware of pedestrians waiting nearby.

Remember, pedestrians are an integral part of our road community, and their safety should be everyone's responsibility.

8.2 Bicyclists

Imagine this scenario: you're cruising down a sunny California road, when suddenly, you see a cyclist pedaling along with you. It's crucial to be aware of these two-wheeled road users and take steps to ensure their safety. Here's what you need to know:

- **Share the Road:** In California, bicycles have the same rights to the road as motor vehicles. Treat cyclists with the same respect and courtesy you would any other vehicle, keeping in mind they have a smaller profile and might need extra space to maneuver safely.
- **Give Ample Passing Distance:** When overtaking a cyclist, leave plenty of room between your vehicle and their bike. California law mandates that drivers must allow at least three feet of clearance when passing a cyclist. This buffer zone ensures their safety and helps to avoid accidents caused by close passing.
- **Patience is a Virtue:** Cyclists might travel at slower speeds than motor vehicles, particularly when ascending a hill or battling against headwinds. Practice patience and wait for a safe opportunity to pass. Avoid honking your horn or driving aggressively to hurry a cyclist along.
- **Check Your Blind Spots:** Cyclists can be harder to spot than larger vehicles, making it vital to double-check your blind spots before changing lanes or making turns. Take an extra moment to ensure there aren't any cyclists nearby before you proceed with your maneuver.
- **Respect Bicycle Lanes and Infrastructure:** Many California roads feature designated bicycle lanes or shared-use paths. Respect these areas and be mindful of cyclists using them. Refrain from parking or stopping in bicycle lanes and yield to cyclists when crossing their designated areas.
- **Watch for Hand Signals:** Cyclists often use hand signals to indicate their intended moves on the road. Familiarize yourself with these signals, such as left turns, right turns, and stopping, to better anticipate their movements and adjust your driving accordingly.
- **Be Careful at Intersections:** Intersections can pose unique challenges for cyclists and drivers to navigate safely. Be vigilant for cyclists before making turns, yield when required, and exercise patience as they navigate through the intersection.

By being mindful and aware of cyclists on the road, we can cultivate a safer environment for everyone to enjoy.

8.3 Motorcyclists

Imagine this: you're cruising down a picturesque California highway, and a motorcycle appears in your rearview mirror. It's crucial to keep an eye out for these two-wheeled speedsters and make an effort to ensure their safety. Here's what you need to remember:

- **Give Them Room:** Motorcycles have every bit as much right to the road as any car, truck, or bus in California. Show them the respect they deserve by providing plenty of room and keeping a safe distance. Remember, motorcycles are nimble and require less space to dart about, so be sure to avoid tailgating or making unexpected lane changes near them.
- **Stay Alert and Aware:** Motorcycles can be a bit trickier to spot than your average vehicle, so extra vigilance is key. Make sure to check your blind spots, use your mirrors regularly, and signal your plans before changing lanes. Be aware that motorcycles can close the gap quickly, so double-check before making any moves.
- **Watch for Hand Signals:** Motorcycles may utilize hand signals, in addition to or instead of their blinkers. Make sure you're familiar with these signals, and keep an eye out for them when you're sharing the road with motorcyclists. This will help you understand their intentions, promoting smoother and safer interactions.
- **Give Extra Time and Space:** Motorcycles have a smaller profile, which can make it harder for them to stand out in traffic. When pulling out of driveways, making a left turn, or navigating intersections, be patient and allow extra time for motorcycles to pass. Give them plenty of room as they might need to swerve or adjust their position to avoid hazards.
- **Use Extra Care at Intersections:** Intersections can be particularly dicey for motorcyclists. Always give a second look for motorcycles before proceeding through an intersection, especially when you're making a left turn. Look out for motorcycles coming from various directions, as their smaller size can make them less noticeable.
- **Mind the Weather:** Remember that motorcycles are more vulnerable to harsh weather conditions. Rain, wind, and other weather elements can affect their stability and visibility. So, in inclement weather, give them extra room and be patient when driving near them.

Remember, sharing the sunny California roads with motorcyclists is part of the journey. Let's ensure it's a safe one for all!

Right Turn*   Slow or Stop   Left Turn

Figure 9: Hand Signals[9]

8.4 School Buses and Emergency Vehicles

Picture this: you're on the move, navigating California's highways when you notice a vibrant, yellow school bus ahead or hear the high-pitched wail of an emergency vehicle. As diligent drivers, it's crucial we know how to share our roads responsibly with these vehicles. Let's dive into some tips for sharing the California roads with school buses and emergency vehicles:

School Buses

When it comes to school buses, ensuring the safety of our precious cargo - the children - is paramount. Here's what you need to know:

- **Halt for Boarding and Disembarking:** When a school bus halts and activates its flashing red lights, it's your cue to stop, regardless of the direction you're heading. This rule holds whether you're on a two-lane road or a highway with multiple lanes. This vital rule ensures the safety of children as they hop on or hop off the bus.
- **Keep a Safe Gap:** It's critical to maintain a safe distance when trailing school buses. This gap allows the bus driver clear visibility and helps avoid accidents in case the bus stops suddenly or makes a turn.
- **Pay Attention in School Zones:** Exercise extra caution when navigating school zones, especially during school hours. Lower your speed, stay alert for children

---

[9] California Driver's Handbook

crossing, and adhere to any posted speed limits or traffic signs in these specially designated areas.

Emergency Vehicles

When emergency vehicles are on an urgent call, we need to ensure their swift and safe passage. Here's what you should do:

- **Pull Over to the Right:** If you spot or hear an emergency vehicle with its sirens and lights on, calmly and safely pull your vehicle over to the right side of the road. If possible, come to a full stop and wait for the emergency vehicle to pass.
- **Avoid Blocking Intersections:** If you're at an intersection and an emergency vehicle is on its way, refrain from entering the intersection and obstructing their path. Instead, hold back until the emergency vehicle has passed before moving ahead.
- **Stay Vigilant and Predictable:** Be on the lookout for emergency vehicles, particularly at intersections or during heavy traffic. Remain calm, signal your intentions, and drive predictably to maintain smooth traffic flow and allow emergency vehicles to navigate safely.

Remember, school buses and emergency vehicles perform essential roles in our communities. By adhering to these guidelines, we can help ensure their operations run safely and smoothly on our roads.

8.5 Large Trucks

Big rigs, 18-wheelers, semi-trucks - those giants of the road! You've seen them cruising along California's highways, right? They're like the arteries of commerce, keeping goods flowing across the state and throughout the country. But sharing the road with them can feel a bit intimidating, can't it? Let's have a chat about doing this safely:

- **Respect the No-Zones:** Large trucks have substantial blind spots or "no-zones", where your vehicle becomes invisible to them. These blind spots usually stretch directly in front, behind, and along the truck's sides, particularly on the right. Here's a rule of thumb: if you can't spot the truck driver in the truck's mirror, they can't see you either. Try to minimize time spent in these no-zones and strive to stay visible to the truck driver.
- **Maintain a Safe Gap:** Think about how long it takes a freight train to halt; large trucks aren't that different. They need more time and space to decelerate or stop compared to your car. So always maintain a safe following distance, and never cut

abruptly in front of a truck then brake suddenly. Believe me, a close encounter with an 18-wheeler's bumper is not on your bucket list!

- **Overtake Thoughtfully:** When you need to overtake a truck, always do so on the left where the truck driver's visibility is best. Make sure you can see the entire truck in your rearview mirror before moving back into your lane. And avoid overtaking while descending a hill—trucks can gather speed here, and you don't want to get drawn into a downhill race!
- **Exercise Patience:** Trucks are bulky, weighty, and not as nimble as your car. They require more time to speed up, more time to slow down, and more room to turn. So, show some patience, offer them the space they need, and remember, the truck drivers are just trying to do their job.
- **Be Ready for Wind Gusts:** Ever been driving next to a big rig when a gust of wind strikes? They can sway and shift unpredictably. Hold your steering wheel firmly and keep your course. The truck driver is doing the same.

Sharing the road with large trucks doesn't have to be intimidating. It's all about understanding how trucks operate and respecting their space on the road. So keep these tips in mind when you encounter a big rig on your next drive.

8.6 Animals

Imagine this: you're gliding along a picturesque California road, enjoying the stunning landscapes and basking in the warm sun. Out of the blue, you spot a stately deer or perhaps a curious squirrel crossing the road. As a responsible driver, it's crucial to know how to share the road safely with our animal friends. Let's delve into some tips on sharing California roads with animals:

- **Stay Alert and Heed Signs:** Keep your eyes wide open and pay attention to any animal crossing signs. These signs are carefully placed in areas known for wildlife activity. By observing these signs, you can anticipate the potential presence of animals and adjust your driving accordingly.
- **Slow Down:** When you approach an area known for wildlife, reduce your speed and drive cautiously. This gives you more time to react if an animal unexpectedly pops up in your path. Remember, animals can be unpredictable, so it's crucial to give yourself ample time to brake or swerve around them if required.
- **Use High Beams at Night:** When driving at night, switch on your high beams whenever it's safe and legal. This increases your visibility and helps you spot

animals along the roadside or crossing the path. However, be mindful of other drivers and switch back to low beams when you see oncoming traffic.

- **Avoid Sudden Swerving:** If you come across an animal in the road, the urge to dodge it is natural. However, swerving suddenly can be hazardous, as it may result in loss of vehicle control or a collision with another car. Instead, brake firmly and, if necessary, steer around the animal while maintaining control of your vehicle.

- **Honk Your Horn:** If an animal is on or near the road but not moving, gently honk your horn. This can encourage the animal to move away from the road, mitigating the risk of a potential collision.

- **Respect Wildlife Crossing Zones:** In certain areas, you might encounter designated wildlife crossing zones or corridors. These zones are intended to offer safe passage for animals. Exercise heightened caution when driving through these zones and allow any crossing animals ample space to do so without disturbance.

Remember, as California drivers, we share our stunning environment with a diverse range of wildlife. By adhering to these tips, we can play our part in protecting both the animals and ourselves on the road. So the next time you meet a creature on your driving adventures, slow down, stay alert, and give them the respect and space they deserve.

9 Driver's License Renewal and Updates

9.1 Renewal Procedures

Time to renew your driver's license, right? Don't sweat it, renewing your license in California isn't as daunting as it might seem. Let's walk through the process:

- **Keep an Eye on the Expiration Date:** First thing's first, note the expiration date on your driver's license. It's crucial to avoid driving with an expired license, okay? In California, driver licenses generally expire every five years on your birthday, but double-checking is always a smart move.
- **Prepare the Necessary Documents:** When it's time to renew, you need to have some key documents at the ready. These typically include proof of identity (like your birth certificate or passport), proof of Social Security number (such as your Social Security card or a W-2 form), and proof of California residency (like a utility bill or lease agreement). Remember to bring these along when you visit the California Department of Motor Vehicles (DMV).
- **Head to the DMV or Renew Online:** When you're ready to renew, you've got two main options: head over to your local DMV office or do it online. If you choose the in-person route, try making an appointment to save time. If you'd rather renew online, make sure you meet certain eligibility criteria, like having a valid credit card and being able to confirm your identity.
- **Pay the Renewal Fee:** Yes, there is a fee to renew your driver's license in California. As of my last update, it's $39.00, but check the DMV website to confirm any updates or changes to the fee amount.
- **Update Your Photo and Information:** The renewal process also allows you to freshen up your photo on your license if you wish. Don't forget to update any changes to your personal information, like your address or name, if needed.

That's the gist of it—how to renew your driver's license in California. It's always best to check the DMV website or call them for the most recent information and additional requirements. Best of luck with your renewal, and stay safe on those roads!

9.2 Address and Name Changes

Moving to a new place or going for a name change? Life is always throwing us curveballs, but the good news is that updating your address or name on your driver's license in California is pretty straightforward. Here's what you need to know:

Address Change

You're settling into your new place, congrats! Now, let's get your driver's license updated with your new address:

- **First off, you'll need some proof of your new address.** This can be a utility bill, lease agreement, or even a voter registration card—anything official that shows your new place.
- **Next, you can update your address either in person at the DMV or online**, if you meet the eligibility requirements. If you choose to go in person, bring your proof of address and be ready to fill out a form.
- **The fee for an address change is currently $28.00**, but always confirm the current fee on the DMV website.
- Once you've updated your address, you'll receive a new driver's license with your updated info. Easy as pie!

Name Change

Let's discuss changing your name on your driver's license. Perhaps you got married, divorced, or decided to change your name for personal reasons. Here's how you do it:

- **Start by collecting some official documents** to support your name change. This could be your marriage certificate, divorce decree, or court-ordered name change document. You'll need these to verify your new name.
- Just like with address updates, **you can change your name at the DMV or online if you're eligible.** If you're visiting in person, bring your official documents and be ready to fill out the necessary forms.
- **Check the DMV website for any fees** related to a name change. As of my last update, the fee was $28.00, but it's always good to double-check the current fee.
- Once you've completed the process and provided the necessary documents, they'll issue a new driver's license with your new name.

Updating your address or name on your driver's license in California is pretty straightforward. Make sure to have the required documents and be prepared to pay any associated fees. So, embrace these changes and let your new driver's license mirror the exciting new chapters of your life!

9.3 Organ Donor and Voter Registration Information

Now, let's talk about some extra decisions you can make related to your driver's license in California—organ donor registration and voter registration. These choices can have a significant impact on others. Let's dive into it!

Organ Donor Registration

Did you know you can be someone's hero even after your time? Registering as an organ donor gives you the power to save lives and offer a second chance. Here's how you can become an organ donor in California:

- When you're renewing your driver's license or getting a new one, the California DMV will ask if you want to register as an organ donor. It's a small question, but the impact is immeasurable.
- By choosing to be an organ donor, you're consenting for your organs and tissues to be used for transplantation or research after your passing. It's a selfless act that can profoundly impact someone else's life.
- You can also register as an organ donor outside of your driver's license renewal by visiting the Donate Life California website (www.donatelifecalifornia.org) to learn more about organ donation in the state.

Voter Registration

Now, let's talk about asserting your democratic rights. Voting is a crucial way to make your voice heard and influence your community. Here's how you can register to vote when renewing your driver's license:

- When at the DMV for your driver's license, they'll ask if you want to register to vote or update your voter registration info. It's an easy way to make sure you're ready to exercise your right to vote.
- If you're not already registered to vote, or if you need to update your info, just say "Yes" and provide the necessary details. The DMV will send your information to the California Secretary of State, and they'll mail you a voter registration card.
- You can also register to vote online through the California Secretary of State's website (www.sos.ca.gov). It's a quick and convenient way to ensure your participation in shaping our democracy.

- Opting to be an organ donor or registering to vote are important choices you can make when getting or renewing your driver's license. By saying "Yes" to organ donation, you can leave a lasting impact and potentially save lives. And by registering to vote, you're asserting your voice and taking part in the democratic process. So, seize these opportunities and let's make a positive impact together!

10 Appendixes

10.1 Glossary of Terms

- **BAC (Blood Alcohol Concentration):** The percentage of alcohol in a person's bloodstream, used to measure intoxication levels.

- **Crosswalk:** A designated area, often marked with painted lines, where pedestrians have the right-of-way to cross the road.

- **Defensive Driving:** A driving technique that involves being aware of potential hazards and taking proactive measures to prevent accidents.

- **DUI (Driving Under the Influence):** Operating a motor vehicle while impaired by alcohol, drugs, or a combination of both.

- **Driver's License:** A legal document issued by the state of California that permits an individual to operate a motor vehicle.

- **HOV (High Occupancy Vehicle) Lane:** A designated lane on certain roads or highways reserved for vehicles with multiple occupants.

- **Learner's Permit:** A restricted license that allows an individual to practice driving under certain conditions before obtaining a full driver's license.

- **Merge:** The process of smoothly blending into traffic when changing lanes or entering a highway from an entrance ramp.

- **No-Fault Insurance:** An insurance system in which each party's insurance company pays for the damages regardless of who is at fault in an accident.

- **Pedestrian:** A person traveling on foot or using a mobility device, such as a wheelchair or scooter, on a roadway or sidewalk.

- **Right-of-Way:** The privilege of proceeding first in a specific situation, often determined by traffic laws and road markings.

- **Road Signs:** Traffic signs and symbols placed along the road to provide information, warnings, and regulations to drivers.

- **Roundabout:** A circular intersection where traffic flows in a counterclockwise direction, and vehicles yield before entering.

- **Speed Limit:** The maximum legal speed at which a vehicle can travel on a specific road or highway.

- **Tailgating:** Driving too closely behind the vehicle in front, which can be dangerous and increase the risk of a collision.

- **Traffic Signal:** A device, typically with red, yellow, and green lights, used to control the flow of traffic at intersections.

- **Turn Signal:** A lever or button inside a vehicle that activates the signal lights to indicate a driver's intention to turn or change lanes.

- **Vision Test:** An examination of an individual's visual acuity to determine if they meet the minimum requirements for driving.

- **Yield:** To give the right-of-way to other vehicles or pedestrians when entering or merging into traffic.

- **Yield Sign:** A triangular-shaped sign that requires drivers to slow down and give the right-of-way to other vehicles or pedestrians.

Made in the USA
Columbia, SC
20 September 2023

23124322R00050